No. 16.—Supplement.

PROFESSIONAL PAPERS

OF THE

CORPS OF ENGINEERS,

UNITED STATES ARMY,

PUBLISHED BY AUTHORITY

OF

THE SECRETARY OF WAR.

HEADQUARTERS CORPS OF ENGINEERS.

1868.

PROFESSIONAL PAPERS, CORPS OF ENGINEERS U. S. A.

No. 16.–Supplement.

SUPPLEMENTARY REPORT

TO

ENGINEER AND ARTILLERY OPERATIONS

AGAINST THE

DEFENCES OF CHARLESTON HARBOR

IN 1863.

By Q. A. GILLMORE,

MAJOR OF ENGINEERS, BREVET MAJOR-GENERAL, U. S. A., LATE MAJOR-GENERAL
OF VOLUNTEERS, AND COMMANDING GENERAL OF THE
U. S. LAND FORCES ENGAGED.

ILLUSTRATED BY SEVEN VIEWS AND PLANS.

NEW YORK:
D. VAN NOSTRAND, 192 BROADWAY.

1868.

TABLE OF CONTENTS.

	PAGE
CONDITION OF FORT SUMTER WHEN CAPTURED, FEBRUARY 18, 1865	5
ARMAMENT OF WORKS, COMPRISING THE DEFENCES OF CHARLESTON AT THE TIME OF ITS CAPTURE, FEBRUARY, 1865	9
CHANNEL OBSTRUCTIONS IN CHARLESTON HARBOR, DURING THE WAR 1861 TO 1865	25
REPORT OF LIEUTENANT TALCOTT, ON CHANNEL OBSTRUCTIONS	27
REPORT OF W. H. DENNIS, ON CHANNEL OBSTRUCTIONS	31
HISTORY OF GUNS EXPENDED	34
JOURNAL OF THE DEFENCE OF FORT SUMTER	41
CONDENSED STATEMENT OF THE CONDITION OF BATTERIES WAGNER AND GREGG, MORRIS ISLAND, JULY 14 TO SEPTEMBER 7, 1863	167

LIST OF VIEWS AND PLANS.

I.—VIEW OF FORT SUMTER, DECEMBER 9, 1863.
II.—CHART OF CHARLESTON HARBOR.
III.—PLAN AND SECTIONS OF FORT SUMTER, AT THE TIME OF ITS CAPTURE, FEBRUARY, 1865.
IV.—PLAN AND SECTIONS OF THE ENEMY'S WORKS ON JAMES ISLAND.
V.—PLAN AND SECTIONS OF ENEMY'S WORKS ON SULLIVAN'S ISLAND.
VI.—PLAN AND SECTIONS OF ENEMY'S WORKS IN CHARLESTON CITY.
VII.—CHANNEL OBSTRUCTIONS.

NOTE.

Major-General Gillmore relieved Major-General Foster of the command of the Department of the South on the 9th of February, 1865. Charleston city and all its defences were evacuated by the enemy on the morning of the 18th February, in consequence of the movement of General W. T. Sherman with his large army in its rear. The co-operative movements of the U. S. forces serving in the Department of the South, consisted in the advance of a column towards Charleston, along the line of the Charleston and Savannah Railroad, under the command of Brigadier-General J. P. Hatch, and of a mixed military and naval force operating from Bull's Bay. The immediate objects of this movement were to force the Christ Church line of works, and then take the Sullivan's Island defences in the rear. The troops were under the immediate command of Brigadier-General E. E. Potter, but, in consequence of unfavorable weather, did not succeed in effecting a landing until a few hours before the evacuation commenced. The confederate troops in retiring set fire to the city in several places, but the flames were extinguished before the conflagration became extensive, by the joint efforts of the U. S. troops and the city firemen. Brigadier-General Schemmelfennig, commanding the U. S. forces on Morris Island, occupied the lower portions of the city before the rear guard of the enemy had left its northern suburbs.

Q. A. G.

CONDITION OF FORT SUMTER,

FEBRUARY, 1865.

THE following description of the condition of Fort Sumter when it came into the possession of the United States forces, February 18, 1865, is deemed sufficiently full to furnish, with the aid of Plates I. and III., a tolerably correct idea of the extent of the demolition to which it was subjected by the fire of our batteries on Morris Island. Plate I. is a perspective bird's eye view of the fort, copied from the captured original bearing General Beauregard's autograph signature of approval. It shows the condition and appearance of the interior of the work, at the close of the autumn of 1863, before any considerable progress had been made by the enemy towards its temporary repair, or towards the construction of bomb-proof shelter, quarters, defensive galleries, etc., for the garrison.

The several figures of Plate III. are drawn from a careful examination of such portions of the works as were not covered up by sand, or otherwise inaccessible.

A full journal of the defence kept by the officers commanding the fort—by Colonel Alfred Rhett to September 4, 1863, and afterwards by Brigadier-General Stephen Elliott—came into our possession by capture, and is inserted in this report.

During the latter part of August, the whole of September, and part of October, 1863, the fort contained no armament with the exception of one old thirty-two-pounder, kept exclusively for firing a sunset gun, in one of the casemates looking up harbor. In October, as soon as the work of covering the casemates on the channel fronts from the reverse fire from Morris Island had become effective, two ten-inch columbiads and one old forty-two-pounder rifle were mounted in the casemates of the northeast front, and remained there until the evacuation, and in February, 1864. One eight-inch and two seven-inch rifles were in like manner mounted in the casemates of the northwest front, but were subsequently removed and taken to the other parts of the harbor.

SUPPLEMENTARY REPORT.

The following description by Major Suter, U. S. Corps of Engineers, is based upon a personal examination of the work made by him in August, 1865:

"The extensive repairs and alterations made by the enemy render
"it difficult to form an exact idea of the damage done to the fort
"by our fire.

"The second tier of casemates have been entirely destroyed, with
"the exception of four casemates on the northwest face, and two
"casemates on the northeast face. On the gorge and southeast faces
"the lower tier of casemates have probably been breached by direct
"fire, but the roofs and partition walls are probably still standing.
"On the north face it is probable that this tier of casemates were
"nearly entirely destroyed by reverse fire. On the northwest and
"northeast faces they are in tolerably good condition. On the north
"face the scarp wall was cut down to the level of the throats of the
"second tier of embrasures. On the northeast and northwest faces
"it is cut down generally to the roofs of the second tier of casemates.
"The upper casemates on these two fronts were destroyed while the
"scarp wall remained standing. The average height of the parapets,
"exposed to direct fire, is 25' above high-water mark.

"The measures resorted to by the enemy to hold the work, after
"it had been virtually destroyed, were to construct extensive and
"secure bomb-proofs under the ruins; to make good communications
"between the different parts of the work; to obstruct, as much as
"possible, the approaches to the work, and to provide means of
"defence in case of an assault. Bomb-proofs were built of 12''
"timber, sheathed with 6'' plank, in rear of the gorge and south-
"east faces. They were apparently placed against the parade wall.
"These bomb-proofs were arranged principally for quarters, having
"chimneys, windows, and ventilators. They were continuous and
"about 330' in length. The width varied from 25 to 10 feet. On
"top was placed 6 to 10 feet of sand. These quarters were loop-
"holed in such a manner that the men could fire from their bunks on
"to the parade of the fort. The commissary storehouse was in the
"bomb-proof on the gorge. On the northwest face, the whole lower
"tier of casemates, and four of the second tier, were converted into
"bomb-proof quarters. Three casemates on the north face were
"included. The casemates were secured from falling in by an in-
"terior shell of wood, arched at the top and strongly shored up with
"heavy timbers. About 8' of earth was placed on the casemate

" roofs, and all breaches in the scarp wall were repaired with gabions.
" The embrasures were left open, affording light and ventilation.
" One gun was mounted in this bomb-proof, bearing towards the city,
" used only for firing the sunset gun. Near it was the principal
" magazine. Near the end of the northeast face are four casemates
" in a good state of preservation. They are closed in rear with
" timbers, and the scarp wall is strengthened with a heavy face cover.
" Three guns are mounted here, bearing toward's Sullivan's Island.
" Earth was placed on top and in rear, making these casemates
" bomb-proof.

" From the north extremity of the gun-chamber runs a small gal-
" lery, opening into a room having loopholes bearing on the parade.
" Above this bomb-proof two casemates of the second tier remain. A
" great deal of earth has been placed on them. In rear of these
" casemates is a wooden bomb-proof. The roof slopes off to the rear,
" leaving an opening in front for the whole length. The earth on
" top is sustained in front by gabions. A ladder leads down from
" this bomb-proof into the gun-room.

" A long gallery leads from the gun-chamber to the bomb-proof in
" the northwest face. This gallery is 4' wide by 8' high. The
" roofs of the casemates are sustained by wooden arches. A similar
" gallery leads from the gun-chamber to the bomb-proof on the south-
" east face.

" Another gallery leads from the southwest face to the bomb-proof
" on the gorge. There are four entrances from the parade to the
" gorge bomb-proof, and two to the southeast bomb-proof.

" The entrance to the fort is on the northwest face. A new dock
" was built here, and a covered gallery $3\frac{1}{2}'$ high and 62' long leads
" through one of the lower embrasures to the inside of the fort.
" This passage is closed at both ends by loopholed doors. In the
" northwest angle a winding flight of stairs leads from the bomb-proof
" to the rampart. In the west angle is a similar staircase. The
" means of egress at the east angle have already been described. On
" the outside is a ramp leading up from the parade to the end of
" the bomb-proof.

" In the south angle the interior of the fort was revetted vertically
" with gabions. A ladder leads from the parade to the rampart.
" The sides of the large bomb-proof, in the centre of the gorge, were
" also revetted vertically with gabions. A ramp and staircase lead
" to the rampart from both sides of this bomb-proof.

"The gorge and southeast faces are arranged for infantry defence. The banquette on the gorge consists generally of a platform of boards. At the east and west angles are small traverses, which were used to cover the five mountain howitzers on the parapet during the day time. They were also occupied by sharpshooters and lookouts. Small magazines for the howitzers are at each extremity of the southeast face. There are also three small traverses at the northwest angle. On the northwest, north, and northeast faces, the debris of the upper casemates has assumed the natural slope, and protects the bomb-proofs and galleries on those faces from reverse fire. On the other two faces, however, a vertical wall of timber or gabions sustains the ruins. About 4' depth of sand has been removed from the parade, and transferred to the ramparts to cover the bomb-proofs, etc."

To provide against assault, a portion of the floating obstructions from the main channel was moved abreast of the northeast front, and the two fronts breached by direct fire from Morris Island. This boom was to prevent the landing of parties from boats upon the ruins of those fronts, which formed one gradual and practicable slope from the crest of the debris to the water's edge. These slopes were also provided with fraize and wire entanglements, as shown on the plan, Plate III.

ARMAMENT OF WORKS

COMPRISING THE DEFENCES OF CHARLESTON AT THE TIME OF ITS CAPTURE, FEBRUARY, 1865.

The following data, derived in part from personal examination, but mainly from reports and surveys by Major Suter, Corps of Engineers, Captain Lüttewitz, 54th New York Vols., and 2d Lieut. Starbird, 55th Mass. Vols., are deemed essentially correct. The drawings of the batteries are in some particulars inaccurate, in giving the calibres of the guns.

FIRST.—Works protecting the city against an attack from the Navy.

a. SULLIVAN'S ISLAND (PLATES II. AND V.)

1. COVE BATTERY.

Armament, four guns.

One 8 in. Columbiad, smooth bore.
Three 6 pdr. field guns.

Two guns command the bridge leading to Mount Pleasant, and two bear on Rebellion Roads and Hog Island Channel; parapet 15 ft. thick, faced on exterior with palmetto logs to resist action of tide; merlons and traverses arranged for musketry defence.

SIGNAL BOMB-PROOF.

Located between Cove Battery and Battery Bee, contains also Engineer offices.

2. BATTERY BEE.

Armament, eleven guns.

Four 10 in. Columbiads, smooth bore.
One   "   "   rifled and banded.
One 11 in. Navy, smooth bore.
One 8 in. Columbiad, "
Four 10 in. Sea-coast mortars.

An open work with circular emplacements for ten heavy guns, and platforms for four mortars, all heavily traversed against Morris Island, and provided with five magazines and two bomb-proof shelters. One of the magazines had been blown up and the gun near it dismounted.

3. BATTERY MARION.

Armament, eight guns.

Three 10 in. Columbiads, smooth bore.
Three 7 in. Brooke rifles.
Two 32 pdrs., rifled and banded (Cal. 6.4).

An open water battery prepared for nine guns, and provided with two magazines and one bomb-proof shelter.

4. MORTAR BATTERY.

Armament, five pieces.

Three 10 in. Sea-coast mortars.
Two 6 pdr. smooth bore iron field-pieces.

5. FORT MOULTRIE.

Armament, nine guns.

Four 10 in. Columbiads, smooth bore.
Two 8 in.   "   "   "
Two 24 pdrs.   "   "
One 32 pdr., rifled and banded (Cal. 6.4).

The scarp wall is banked up with sand on the exterior, and bomb-proofs and magazines have been built inside the work.

6. MORTAR BATTERY.

Adjacent to Fort Moultrie on the east is a battery mounting

Two 10 in. Sea-coast mortars.

7. BATTERY RUTLEDGE.

Armament, six guns.

Three 10 in. Columbiads, smooth bore.
One 10 in.   "   rifled and banded.
Two 6 pdr. smooth bore iron field-pieces.

This work is provided with a bomb-proof and magazine. Battery Rutledge is connected with the next battery to the eastward, mounting heavy guns, by a parapet, behind which is mounted six field-pieces provided with one magazine.

Armament.

Two 12 pdr. smooth bore, iron.
Four 6 pdr.   "   "   "

8. Fort Beauregard.

Armament, thirteen guns.

One 10 in. Columbiad, smooth bore.
One 8 in.   "   rifled and banded.
Three 8 in. Sea-coast howitzers.
Three 32 pdrs., rifled and banded.
One 32 pdr., smooth bore.
Two 24 pdrs.,   "   "
One 6 pdr., smooth bore iron field-piece.
One 6 pdr., rifled   "   "

This work is enclosed, and the eastern front extends entirely across the island, thus closing the approach from that direction.

Inclined palisading and wire entanglements are placed along the front of several of the above-named works, beginning at the right of Fort Moultrie, and ending at the left of the eastern front of Fort Beauregard, near the marsh.

9. Two Gun Batteries.

Between Fort Beauregard and Fort Marshall, located on the eastern extremity of Sullivan's Island, are four detached batteries, each mounting two guns, as follows:

No. 1. Two 32 pdr., smooth bore.
No. 2. Two   "   "   "
No. 3. Two 24 pdrs. "   "
No. 4. Two   "   "   "

10. Fort Marshall.

Armament, fourteen guns.

One 24 pdr. siege, smooth bore.
One 32 pdr., rifled and banded.
One 8 in. Columbiad, smooth bore.
Three 8 in. Sea-coast howitzers.
Two 12 pdr. iron rifles.
One 7 in. Brooke rifle.
One 4 in. Blakely rifle.
One 8 in. Navy shell gun.
One 12 pdr. iron smooth bore.
Two 6 pdr. iron smooth bore.

A portion of this armament is in an enclosed work, of which the parapets are 25 feet in height and 15 feet thick. It is provided with a bomb-proof of great capacity, and is entered through a covered gateway in the rear face. The outworks extend to the extreme north end of the island, to guard against assault from Long Island.

b. CHRIST CHURCH PARISH.

1. Beach Batteries No. 1 and No. 2.

Armament.

No. 1. One 32 pdr., smooth bore.
No. 2. One 32 " rifled and banded.

Located on the main land on the edge of the marsh abreast of Sullivan's and Long Islands, to command the creeks emptying into Breach Inlet.

2. Battery Gary.

Armament.

Two 8 in. rifles.

Located on the Mount Pleasant shore, and command the bridge leading to Sullivan's Island, as well as the entrance to Hog Island Channel.

3. Hog Island Battery.

Never Armed.

On southern shore of Hog Island, and provided with magazine and bomb-proof shelter.

4. Hobcaw Point Battery.

Never Armed.

A work for two guns to command Cooper and Wando Rivers.

5. CASTLE PINCKNEY.

Armament.

Three 10 in. Columbiads, smooth bore.
One 7 in. Brooke Rifle.

An old permanent work on Shute's Folly Island, one mile east of the city. The scarp wall is protected by piling sand against it to the thickness of over 20 feet. Has two magazines and a bomb-proof shelter. Its guns cover the harbor from Mount Pleasant to James Island.

6. FORT RIPLEY.

Never Armed.

A small work for two guns, built on the "Middle Ground," upon a crib work of pine logs, faced on the outside with palmetto logs. Used as a signal station.

c. CITY BATTERIES.

1. CALHOUN ST. BATTERY.

Armament.

One 8 in. rifle, banded.

2. LAURENS ST. BATTERY.

Armament.

One 10 in. Columbiad, smooth bore.

3. CUSTOM HOUSE BATTERY.

Armament.

One 13 in. Blakely Rifle, burst by the enemy on the morning of the evacuation.

4. VANDERHORST WHARF BATTERY.

Armament, two guns.

One 10 in. Columbiad, smooth bore.
One 42 pdr., rifled and banded.

The battery was never entirely finished.

5. BATTERY RAMSAY.

Armament, six guns.

The eastern portion mounted
> One 13 in. Blakely rifle (bursted by the enemy).
> Two 10 in. Columbiads, smooth bore.
> One 11 in. Navy gun.

The southern portion mounted
> One 10 in. Columbiad, smooth bore.
> One 42 pdr., rifled and banded.

Located at White Point Garden, and bearing on the inner harbor and on Ashley River.

6. BATTERY WARING.

Armament.

Two 10 in. Columbiads, smooth bore.

Located south of Chisholm's Mills, and commanded Ashley River.

d. JAMES ISLAND.

1. BATTERY MEANS.

No armament.

An open battery, located about 800 yards east of the pontoon bridge over Wappoo Creek, to command the débouche of that stream. The platforms are for siege guns.

2. BATTERY GLOVER.

Armament.

Three 8 in. rifles.

A open battery on Ashley River with a wet ditch on the front and flanks, and provided with a magazine and a large bomb-proof.

3. BATTERY WAMPLER.

Armament.

Two 10 in. Columbiads, smooth bore.

On Ashley River, about three-quarters of a mile west of Fort Johnson. Its guns cover the inner harbor as far west as Castle Pinckney.

4. FORT JOHNSON.

Armament.

Water Battery. { One 10 in. Columbiad, rifled and banded.
Two 10 in.   "   smooth bore.
One 42 pdr.   "   rifled and banded.

Extreme Left. Four 10 in. Columbiads, smooth bore.

Flanking Guns. { Eight field pieces.
One 8 in. siege howitzer.

One 32 pdr., rifled and banded.
Two 10 in. Sea-coast mortars.

This work, with its outworks, forms an intrench camp of considerable strength and capacity.

On the extreme point a water battery of four guns sweep the harbor from Sumter to Ripley inclusive. These guns are in circular chambers, with traverses between them 30 ft. long, 20 ft. wide, and 10 ft. high, and lapping over the parapet so as to form deep embrasures, and give entire protection against our batteries on Morris Island. To the left along the shore a thick infantry parapet connects the Water Battery with another open battery of four smooth-bore Columbiads, mounted in deep circular chambers, connected by narrow covered passageways (a method of construction common to many of the batteries around Charleston), while on the right, along the beach, is a heavy traverse containing a capacious bomb-proof shelter, flanked by an 8 in. howitzer on the parapet of the Water Battery. Still further to the right an infantry parapet with a feeble abatis in front, and flanked at intervals with eight field-pieces mounted in caponniers and indents, extends across Simkins' neck, following the edge of the marsh to a bluff where the right of the line rests. In rear of this point is a high battery mounting one 32 pdr., rifled and banded; and between this and the four-gun battery on the extreme left is a bomb-proof shelter.

5. SIMKINS' BATTERIES.

Armament.

No. 1. One 10 in. Columbiad, rifled and banded.
No. 2. One 10 in. Sea-coast mortar.
No. 3. Two   "   "   "
No. 4. Two 8 in. Sea-coast howitzers.

These batteries are located on the shell beach southeast from Fort Johnson, and are connected with the latter and with each other by a shallow rifle-pit.

e. 6. FORT SUMTER.

Armament.

One 32 pdr., used as a sunset gun only.
Two 10 in. Columbiads, smooth bore.
One 7 in. rifle.

Five mountain howitzers (12 pdrs.) mounted on the parapet to repel assaults.

The condition of this work is fully described in another portion of this report.

SECOND.—Defensive Works to Repel an Attack by Land Forces.

a. 1. CHRIST CHURCH PARISH.

The approach from the northeast by way of Bull's Bay, down the peninsula formed by Cooper and Wandoo River on one side and the ocean on the other, is closed by a continuous line of intrenchments, with its flanks resting on impracticable marshes.

Armament.

Palmetto Battery, on the right,
  One 9 in. Navy shell gun.
  Two 32 pdrs., rifled and banded.

At the centre near 6 Mile Church,
  Two 20 pdrs., Parrott rifles.

At the left on Elliott's Creek,
  Two 32 pdrs., smooth bore.

The line is provided with capponiers and indents, having platforms for flanking field-pieces, but no guns.
The parapet is about 6 ft. high, and 10 ft. to 14 ft. thick.
The ditch in front is sunk below low water.

SUPPLEMENTARY REPORT.

b. 2. ST. JAMES'—GOOSE CREEK—PARISH.

Armament, six guns.

Two 32 pdrs., smooth bore.
Four 24 pdrs., brass howitzers.

Major Suter describes this line as follows:

" The approaches along Charleston neck are defended by a line of
" works, just outside the city limits. The right rests on Magnolia
" Cemetery on Cooper's River; the left rests on the marsh, near
" Racker's Mills, on Ashley River. The high-road and railroad pass
" through openings left in the line.

" At the centre of the line are two bastioned fronts, with outworks.
" The tracé is the same as laid down for permanent works, all the
" details being followed out with farcical minuteness. Owing, how-
" ever, to the shortness of the fronts, and the want of profile (the
" ditches are not more than 4 ft. deep), the outworks are cramped
" and not properly commanded by the enceinte. They would prob-
" ably be of more assistance to an attacking party than to the gar-
" rison.

" From these fronts an indented line runs to both rivers. The
" flanks bear towards the centre.

" The ground in front of these works is low, and the ditches are
" partially wet.

" There were four brick magazines along the line and platforms for
" 14 guns.

" There were no obstacles in front of the line."

c. 3. ST. ANDREW'S PARISH,

(Between Ashley River, Wappoo Creek, and Stono River.)

The approach between Ashley and Stono Rivers is defended by a line of nine detached batteries, the right resting behind a marshy creek about one mile south of Ashley, and the left near the elbow of the Stono next above Fort Pemberton. This is a strong line, as the marshes in its front are almost impassable, and mounted twenty-two guns when captured.

The two works near the railroad are enclosed.

The approach to Ashley Ferry on the right front is closed by a four-bastioned work located about one thousand yards southwest of the ferry, prepared for sixteen guns, and provided with a magazine and bomb-proof.

In front of Ashley River bridge two square redoubts are located, one for six and the other for seven guns, to command the railroad and county road and the bridges over Wappoo Creek. These works are covered in front by a line of rifle-pits.

Of this line, only the two enclosed works on the railroad, about five miles from the city, were permanently garrisoned.

d. JAMES ISLAND.

The communication between James Island and the main land lying between Ashley and Stono Rivers, was maintained by means of two drawbridges over Wappoo Creek, located at distances of about one mile and a half from Ashley, and by permanent bridges over the creek or cut near the Stono, all of which were destroyed by the enemy before evacuation.

1. FORT PEMBERTON.

Armament removed by the Enemy.

This is a closed pentagonal work located on the left bank of the Stono, and besides constituting a part of the defences against an attack by land forces, is specially intended to resist the advance of a fleet up Stono River. The work has two magazines and a hot-shot furnace (Plates II. and IV.).

2. INTERIOR DEFENSIVE LINE.

The right of this line rests on Wappoo Creek, about one mile in rear of Fort Pemberton, and runs thence south about one mile and a quarter to the road leading to Fort Pemberton, thence east about three-quarters of a mile crossing a branch of James Island Creek, to the creek itself. It is made up of straight lines of infantry parapet, flanked by field-pieces in the salients of irregular redans.

In rear of the "branch" the position is strengthened by a square redoubt with faces 60 yards long, and in rear of the right of the line, and south of the drawbridge over Wappoo Creek, is an open battery commanding the bend of the creek. Communication with the part of the island south of James Island Creek is maintained by three permanent bridges—one about three-quarters of a mile south of the square redoubt on the Fort Pemberton road, another about three-quarters of a mile east of the redoubt, and the third still further to the east at Dale's Bluff.

On the right bank of James Island Creek, about a mile and a half east of the redoubt—which interval is covered mostly by creeks and marshes—the works are resumed again, running in a southeasterly direction about two miles to Clark's Point. They consist essentially of six square redoubts for two guns (faces 60 yards), flanked in the intervals by irregular redans for one gun (faces 40 to 50 yards). The right half of this line, located behind a swamp, consisted of detached gun batteries connected by rifle-pits.

All the works from James Island Creek to Clark's Point were in bad condition, the dependence being chiefly upon the "siege line" in advance, which was of more recent construction. The Clark's Point Redoubt was kept in repair. Two field guns were found there, and platforms for two others were in order. From this point the line runs along Light House Creek to the northeast, comprising—

Battery Ryan—on the Right.

Armament.

One 8 in. siege howitzer.
Three 24 pdr. howitzers (brass).

Battery Ryan—on the Left.

Armament.

Two 32 pdr. howitzers.
One 24 pdr. brass howitzer.

A line of rifle-pits, 600 yards long, armed with three field-pieces, connects Battery Ryan with

Battery Tatam.

This work was prepared for five light guns, and provided with a large bomb-proof shelter. A line of palisading runs in front of the two batteries Ryan and Battery Tatam. To the left of Tatam a line of rifle-pits, armed with two field-pieces, extends to

Battery Haskell.

This is a massive open work prepared for twelve guns, in circular or polygonal chambers, with a parapet 18 ft. thick and 15 ft. high. Many of the guns had two embrasures. To the left a line of rifle-pits connects with a battery for two mortars, with a magazine in rear.

The guns left in this work were—

    One 8 in. Navy shell gun.
    One 32 pdr., smooth bore.
    Two 10 in. Sea-coast mortars.

Battery Cheves.

The left of this line, and connecting it with the channel bearing the works, is Battery Cheves, located on a high bank about midway between Battery Haskell and Fort Johnson. It is provided with a magazine and bomb-proof, and armed with one 10 in. and one 8 in. smooth-bore Columbiad, with platforms for two other guns.

3. Exterior or "Siege" Line.

This line of works was constructed at a later period than the Interior Line, was much more advantageously located, and was, therefore, the chief reliance for defence. Its right, at Battery Tynes, rests on the Stono about two miles and a half south of Fort Pemberton, while its left envelopes the village of Secessionville—the scene of Brigadier-General Benham's attack in 1862—almost surrounded by swamps, and located directly upon the deep creeks and bayoux emptying into Folly River and Light House Inlet.

Battery Tynes.

Armament.

    Two 8 in. Columbiads, rifled and banded.
    Two 32 pdrs.,   "   "

Located on the Stono, and commanding the bridge leading to John's Island. Prepared for five guns, and provided with a large magazine and bomb-proof shelter.

BATTERY PRINGLE.

Armament.

Two 10 in. Columbiads, smooth bore.
One 8 in.   "   "   "
Three 42 pdrs., rifled and banded.
One 32 pdr.,   "   "
Two 6 pdrs., iron field guns.

Located on the Stono, and with Battery Tynes intended to take the place of Fort Pemberton, and prevent the siege line being turned by a mixed force ascending the Stono. It has a strong water battery prepared for nine heavy guns, and commands Stono River, John's Island, and the front of the siege line. The guns are separated by heavy traverses.

Between Batteries Tynes and Pringle, a permanent bridge crosses the Stono, communicating with firm ground on John's Island by a long causeway secured by a tête-de-pont, called

FORT TRENHOLM.

Armament.

Two 8 in. Columbiads, smooth bore.
Two 10 in.   "   "   "
Two 42 pdrs., rifled and banded.
One 32   "   "   "
One 24   "   "   "
Two Navy 32 pdrs., smooth bore.
One 24 pdr., smooth bore, siege.
One 8 in. siege howitzer.
Two 6 pdr. smooth-bore field guns.

Two fronts of the work, looking down the Stono and towards Legareville, are bastioned, terminating in an indented line which runs to the edge of the marsh. The southeast front is connected with the marsh in a similar manner. The gorge of the work is open.

The work was prepared for seventeen guns, fourteen of which were left by the enemy.

About two hundred yards in rear of Trenholm is a small open two gun battery for protecting the causeway.

It mounted two 6 pdr. field-pieces.

This battery sweeps the parade of Trenholm, and both are well commanded by the guns of Batteries Pringle and Tynes.

BATTERY LEROY.

Armament.

Two 8 in. Navy shell guns.
One 10 in. Sea-coast mortar.
One 32 pdr. gun, rifled and banded (3½ ft. of chase cut off and gun used as a rifled mortar).

Battery Leroy is a redan, about 400 yards east of Battery Pringle; thence an indented line 385 yds. long leads to

BATTERY No. 1.

Armament.

One 8 in. Sea-coast howitzer.
Two 24 pdr. guns, smooth bore.
One 18 "   "   "   "
One 12 pdr. iron field gun, smooth bore.

This battery is a redan with a magazine, and is prepared for seven guns.

To the left, an indented line, 800 yards long, with eight salients, leads to

BATTERY No. 2.

Mounting One 8 in. Navy shell gun.
One 8 in. Sea-coast howitzer.
Two 32 pdr. guns, smooth bore.
One 24 pdr.   "   "   "

This is similar in form to No. 1, is prepared for seven guns, has a signal and telegraph station, and is connected with the next work on the left by an indented line 600 yards long.

BATTERY No. 3.

Mounting One 32 pdr. gun, smooth bore.
Two 24 "   "   "   "
Two 18 "   "   "   "

Prepared for seven guns, and similar to Nos. 1 and 2.

SUPPLEMENTARY REPORT.

An indented line, 460 yards long, with three salients, leads to

BATTERY No. 4,

Similar to No. 3, and

Mounting One 8 in. Sea-coast howitzer.
One 32 pdr. smooth-bore gun.
One 32 pdr. howitzer.
One 24 pdr. smooth-bore gun.

An indented line, 550 yards long, with four salients, connects it with

BATTERY No. 5.

Mounting One 12 pdr. English gun.
Two 24 pdr. guns, smooth bore.
One 8 in. brass howitzer.

Similar in form to those above named.

A parapet with five salients connects it with the creek in rear and north of Secessionville.

The timber in front of the line between Battery No. 5 and Battery Pringle was felled and formed a good abatis. In the intervals between the main works, platforms for field guns were laid. Twenty-seven guns were found on this line. The works were all well constructed and kept in good repair.

SECESSIONVILLE WORKS.

These form a large entrenched camp, the only approach to which, from the front, is by a narrow neck of land held by

BATTERY LAMAR.

Armament.

One 42 pdr., rifled and banded.
Three 8 in. siege howitzers.
One 24 pdr. smooth-bore siege gun.

This work is provided with a magazine and a large bomb-proof.

SECESSIONVILLE WATER BATTERIES.

Armament.

Three 32 pdr. guns, rifled and banded.
One 24 pdr.   "   "   "
One 24 pdr. rifle.
Two 32 pdr. Navy smooth bores.
Two 32 pdr. Navy howitzers.
One 24 pdr. iron howitzer.
Two 6 pdr. iron field guns, smooth bore.

These works extend from the left of Battery Lamar, along the edge of the marsh, to the bridge leading to Clark's Point. The line is indented, and has one bomb-proof shelter and two magazines. The guns bear on Black and Long Islands and the creeks adjacent thereto.

A line of rifle-pits runs across the marsh and water to Clark's Point, to prevent boat parties from landing in rear of the siege line.

CHANNEL OBSTRUCTIONS IN CHARLESTON HARBOR,

DURING THE WAR 1861 TO 1865.

The popular ideas which pervaded the public mind, and even influenced and directed official action, with regard to those mysterious channel obstructions alleged to be in extensive use by the enemy, as passive auxiliaries in the defence of the city and harbor of Charleston in 1863 and 1864, were singularly exaggerated and incorrect.

The opinion entertained at that time by many practical men, whose official and professional relations required them to think upon the subject, that there was much in them that was purely mythical, has been fully vindicated and confirmed.

Brigadier-General Ripley, who had immediate command of the troops engaged in the defence of Charleston, and other officers of the confederate service whose position enabled them to speak from positive knowledge, have, since the close of the war, given some interesting information upon this question.

From their statements, many of which are written, it has been ascertained that it was the constant and studied practice of the confederate commanders to circulate exaggerated and erroneous reports concerning the means of defence, and that to such an extent and with such skill was this ruse made use of, that with few exceptions, neither the inhabitants of the city, nor the troops defending it, possessed any correct knowledge of the channel obstructions.

Such a semblance of necessary and systematic labor in their construction, management, and repair, was kept up, and such an affectation of secrecy concerning their real character, and of confidence in their efficiency was assumed, in order to keep all knowledge or suspicion of the huge fiction from us, that the blockade runners themselves knew almost nothing of the really harmless character of the hidden obstructions they were told to avoid.

A credulous commander of a foreign man-of-war, who in the year 1863 was permitted to go up to the city in a small boat, returned to his ship outside the bar, with the most extravagant admiration for the formidable character of the existing arrangements for submarine defence; and although he had really seen next to nothing, reported the entire harbor to be literally filled with fixed and floating obstructions, and subaqueous mines and torpedoes.

The obstructions, therefore, feeble and incomplete as they were, secured to the enemy all the practical results of a thorough and effective system, inasmuch as their supposed strength, it is presumed, prevented any attempt being made by our monitors to run by them.

When the city came into our possession, on the 18th of February, 1865, and the novel spectacle was presented of a large fleet, including gunboats, army and navy transports, tugs, and sutlers' vessels, passing up to the city and dispersing themselves over the inner waters of the harbor, without encountering, except in one isolated and harmless instance, any of those hidden dangers, of which the existence had been so often reported, and by many so persistently believed, the question very naturally arose, whether, at any previous time during the war, the passive obstacles to an entrance, such as fixed and floating obstructions and torpedoes, had been in reality more formidable than we found them at that late period.

Many thinking men had entertained the belief that the practice of running the blockade at night, which was constantly and successfully carried on at Charleston throughout the years 1863 and 1864, was certain evidence of the existence of a wide and practicable channel up to the city, and it was presumed that the professional services of the masters and pilots of those blockade runners which had been captured, might be made available whenever our fleet should make the attempt to run in.

Moreover, steamers bearing flags of truce had, not unfrequently, come down near our fleet and returned to the city in the day time, and the route they took was quite well understood.

Efforts have been made to procure full and correct information upon this subject from officers and employees of the late confederate service.

It is hoped that any official and original plans and reports in existence, giving information of these obstructions, will be published to the world.

In pursuing the investigations, many persons familiar with the subject were consulted, and a correspondence was entered into with certain officers of high rank in the late confederate service most likely to be possessed of trustworthy information.

The utmost care has been taken to exclude all but well-authenticated data.

SUPPLEMENTARY REPORT.

From the concurrent testimony thus procured, it appears that *there was nothing in the shape of channel obstructions or torpedoes that could prevent or seriously retard the passage of our fleet up to Charleston city or above it, in 1863 and 1864, by using the channel left open for blockade runners; that such channel obstructions and torpedoes as did exist, were not regarded by the enemy as at all formidable, or likely to afford them much protection in the event of an actual attack; and that at no time during the war was their condition any better, or their efficiency any more to be relied on, to delay the passage of a fleet, than when the city came into our possession in February,* 1865.

The following reports of Lieutenant Talcott and Mr. Wm. H. Dennis are believed to be correct in all essential particulars, having been examined and corroborated by officers of the confederate army engaged in the defence of Charleston during the period to which they refer:

HEADQUARTERS, DEPARTMENT OF THE SOUTH,
HILTON HEAD, S. C., April 12, 1865.

Major-General Q. A. GILLMORE,
   Commanding Department of the South,
      Hilton Head, S. C.

GENERAL,—In compliance with instructions received from you, I have the honor to submit the following report concerning the obstructions which have been and now are in existence in Charleston Harbor. The information embodied in the report has been derived in part from the evidence of citizens of Charleston, who have been concerned, directly or indirectly, with the obstructions, and partly from my own observations.

The first obstruction was placed across the channel between Forts Sumter and Moultrie, on or near the line marked A B on the chart, and was put in position in the latter part of 1861, soon after the capture of Port Royal by the United States forces. It consisted of a framed timber raft, Fig. 1, Plate VII., made of 12 in. or 14 in. square timbers, bolted together, built in sections, and coupled together with chain couplings at C D. It was anchored with ships' anchors at short intervals, both up and down stream. The ends of the cross timbers

E F were pointed. A chain A B was wound under and over the centre timber, running the whole length of the raft. It never extended entirely across the channel, a passage-way always existing next Fort Sumter. By the time it was all put down, it had commenced to break away, and was entirely abandoned in this position in December, 1861, or the early part of 1862. The sections were then towed up the harbor and anchored across Folly channel. The piling now remaining there was driven to confine this timber raft, and prevent it from drifting. It was afterwards entirely given up, and only the piling now stands.

After this obstruction was abandoned between Forts Sumter and Moultrie, it was replaced by what was known as the railroad iron obstructions, Fig. 2, Plate VII. They were made of four timbers A B, about twelve inches square, bound together with iron bands E E E. At G G an iron bolt was passed through the timber, the lower end being provided with an eye, in which a bar of railroad iron C D was secured, the timber serving as a float. The sections were the length of a bar of railroad iron, and were coupled with chain couplings at the ends of the rails. It was anchored at every coupling alternately up and down stream. It extended at first in a continuous line from Fort Sumter to Fort Moultrie, excepting the ship channel next Fort Sumter, which was left open. It was found impossible to hold it in its place in this position, and it was afterwards anchored in sections of 200 feet in length, arranged as in Fig. 3, Plate VII. This obstruction remained in one shape or another until the early part of 1863, when it was towed away to obstruct the creeks about Charleston, where it had not so much current to contend with.

A rope obstruction was next put down in the same location. This consisted of three cables of different sizes, the largest of from six-inch to nine-inch rope, and the others of six-inch, four-inch, and three-inch rope. The upper and largest one had barrel buoys (Fig. 4, Pl. VII.) attached to float the obstruction. The three cables were rattled together like the rigging of a ship, as represented in the figure. Attached to the floating cable were entangling lines hanging loosely from buoy to buoy, intended for fouling the propellers of vessels attempting to run by. Entangling lines of about 15 ft. in length, and confined at one end only, also swung from the lower cable for the same purpose. The obstruction was anchored with ordinary anchors from the lower cable, and swung with the tide, forming an arc of a circle up or down stream, as the current chanced to be moving. At first it was placed in a continuous line across the channel, but after parting once or twice from collisions and the force of the current, it was cut up and anchored in sections in the same way as the railroad iron obstruction.

One or two of the blockade runners fouled in it, but experienced no material inconvenience, it being easily cut away. It was in position at the time of the naval attack upon Fort Sumter, April 7, 1863, and one of the monitors carried away a part of it in her propeller. It was abandoned in the fall of 1863, as impracticable. As was the case with the other obstructions, a channel always existed on the side nearest Fort Sumter, passable by vessels of heavy draught. A rope obstruction, differing somewhat from the preceding one, was placed between Forts Sumter and Moultrie, in December, 1864, and January, 1865. It consisted of single cables (A B, Fig. 5, Pl. VII.), about one hundred feet long, made with an eye at one end and supported by log buoys. To this cable were attached entangling lines, E E. The sections were anchored at one end only, and swung with the tide. They were arranged in two parallel lines, the sections being one hundred feet apart, and the lines one hundred feet apart, as shown in Fig. 6, Pl. VII. I think that some of them were still remaining when the United States forces occupied Charleston in February, 1865. They never extended over more than two-thirds the distance from Fort Sumter to Fort Moultrie, and never covered the ship channel next Fort Sumter.

In January, 1865, there were sixteen barrel torpedoes placed between Forts Sumter and Moultrie, extending across the main ship channel. They were anchored with a single mushroom anchor to each, with such length of rope as to leave them four or five feet below the surface of the water at low tide. The last ones were placed the night that the monitor Patapsco was destroyed, and she was blown up by one of them. Nine of the sixteen have since been exploded or taken up. Some of the others have probably broken loose and gone adrift. The U. S. Coast Survey Steamer Bibb exploded one in March, 1865, *without damage*, while running the main ship channel in twenty-nine feet of water. Seven were also placed in Rebellion Roads, on a line from Castle Pinckney to Battery Bee. There were also three large boiler-iron torpedoes placed, one off Fort Wagner at the spot marked L on the chart, one in Rebellion Roads and one in Ashley River off White's Point. It was intended that they should be exploded by a galvanic battery from the shore, but the exploding cables were broken in placing them, and they were thereby rendered useless.

The only other obstructions in the harbor of which I could find any trace, were in the shape of torpedo rafts. These were composed of four round logs (Figs. 7 and 8, Pl. VII.) sixty feet long, and about five feet from the lower end a square timber F F was bolted on the upper side to bind them together. Ten feet from the upper end, three timbers C D, about fourteen inches square, were bolted to the lower side as floats. Cast-iron torpedoes G G, capable of containing from twenty-five to fifty pounds of powder, were fastened on to the upper ends of the timbers, and at right angles to them. The rafts were anchored inclining up stream, as shown in Fig. 8, so as to leave the torpedoes about three feet below the surface of the water at low tide, one anchor, I, leading from the lower end, and one, H, from the float timbers. The enemy's steamer Marion ran upon one of these rafts in Ashley river, in April, 1863, exploding two of the torpedoes and sinking her at once. Four sections were put down in Ashley River, opposite the Bath House, at right angles to the channel, on the line marked M N on the chart, three sections in Hog Island channel, on the line F G, and three across the slough on the line I H. One section lies at present half immersed in the water, along side the Palmetto dock on Cooper River.

The testimony of all the parties whom I examined agrees as regards the practicability of entering the harbor, so far as obstructions were concerned, at any time previous to November or December, 1864. The pilot of the Palmetto State (enemy's gunboat) states, that on the night of the 7th April, 1863, after the naval attack upon Fort Sumter, he took that vessel drawing thirteen feet of water down outside of Fort Sumter, and that although the night was very dark, and he had not run the channel for some time, he kept the south or main ship channel and found no obstructions. A pilot who has been in the harbor during the entire war says, that before the torpedoes were put down in the winter of 1864–5, he would have had no hesitation, from fear of any obstructions, in taking any vessel which would come over the bar, up to the city, following the main ship channel. One of the blockade runner pilots, who has frequently run them into Charleston, says, that even after the torpedoes were placed, he has brought in, in the night, a vessel drawing ten feet of water, running from Sullivan's Island to the channel next Fort Sumter to clear the rope obstructions, and passing over the torpedo ground without any specific information as to their location, without even touching them. All parties agree that the only danger to be apprehended was from the enemy's shore batteries. My informants state, that after Fort Sumter was reduced from Morris Island, in August, 1863, it was expected that the iron-clads would come up to the city, and that they were ridiculed by every one for not attempting it, at the least. It seems also that the channel next Fort Sumter was never really obstructed until the torpedoes were put down in the winter of 1864–5. While the three first-described obstructions were across the channel, a section was always kept in reserve to close up the gap, but it was anchored near Fort Johnson, and a vigorous push would have passed Fort Sumter before they could have placed it.

Those conversant with the force of the current between Forts Sumter and Moultrie are of the opinion that the only danger to be apprehended from the torpedoes placed there was just at slack water, as either upon the ebb or flood tide the current would keep them so far below the surface of the water as to prevent the possibility of any vessel touching them.

I am, General,
Very respectfully, your obedient servant,
(Signed)   ED. N. KIRK TALCOTT,
Lieut. 1st N. Y. Engineers.

CHARLESTON, August 3, 1865.

The foregoing report is correct as far as relates to the obstructions in this harbor during the war. There are slight errors in regard to dates, and also the object and character of the obstructions commenced with piles and rafts between Castle Pinckney and Fort Johnson. The work was, however, never completed, and they are immaterial.
(Signed)   R. S. RIPLEY.

U. S. SCHOONER "CASWELL,"
OFF CHARLESTON HARBOR,
March 17, 1865.

SIR,—Agreeable to your instructions of March 1st, in reference to the obstructions in Charleston harbor, I have to make the following report, based on information from residents of Charleston (and principally from one Captain Revel, who commanded the steamer Chesterfield, which assisted in laying the obstructions), and from my own observations. The first line, marked A B (on the chart), was laid soon after the capture of Port Royal, and is known as the "raft obstructions," was constructed of a frame work of timber bolted together, and the sections made fast to each other by a chain. A chain also run the entire length of the raft, being wound under and over the middle timber. This raft was anchored, with anchors and chains at short distances from each other, both up and down stream. The raft remained for about two months, when it was broken up by an easterly gale, and was left swinging with the tide, offering no obstruction to navigation in daylight, as it could be easily run, and there being room between the sections for vessels to run. It was subsequently taken up, and one part towed in front of Fort Sumter (O P on chart), the other was placed between the piling J K, which crosses Folly Island and Hog Island channels. It disappeared entirely in a short time. A second line was placed across the harbor at A C. This was constructed of timber and railroad iron, the iron being surrounded by four twelve-inch timbers, and made secure by straps of iron round the whole; at the ends of railroad iron an eye was made, through which a link (of two and a half inch iron) about eight inches diameter passed, securing them together. This obstruction did not remain so long as the first, but soon broke apart, and being anchored as the first, swung as that one did after breaking, with the tide. In February, 1864, two hundred and seventy feet of it came ashore at Folly Island, and I am informed that it entirely disappeared about that time. In March 1863, the third line, known as the rope obstruction, was placed in the harbor, on the line D E. This was constructed of six-inch rope, of which there were three strands wattled together as the shrouds of a vessel, and kept afloat by barrel buoys. Soon after this line was put down a blockade runner ran into it, but succeeded in getting through after cutting the line, and like the others it was left to swing with the tide; some fathoms of it were carried away by one of the monitors after the attack on the 7th of April, 1863, and from reports here it disappeared soon after. At the same time the rope obstructions were put down, there were several torpedoes placed in the channels. The first of boiler iron, in six fathoms of water, about E. by N. from Fort Wagner. This was to be exploded by galvanic action, through wire from Battery Gregg, but was not successful, and is undoubtedly floating about the vicinity now, but rendered harmless by the wire being disconnected. A second similar to this was placed in Rebellion Road, at R, the wire of which ran to Battery Bee. The third of this description, placed off White's Point, was removed soon after. There were also some torpedoes or shell-rafts placed in the harbor. The rafts were of three pieces of timber about thirty feet in length each, and fifteen feet between, with two cross timbers, one at the lower end and the other half way from there to the points on which were placed cast-iron shells. These were anchored, inclined up stream, with the shells two feet under water at low tide. Three of these rafts were anchored on the line H I, two in front of the obstructions in Hog Island channel F G, and three at the mouth of Ashley river, on the line M N. One of these blew up the Confederate steamer Marion. Hog Island and Folly Island channels were obstructed by piles driven on the line J K, many of which are still standing. In all the obstructions thus far, a channel was left open on Fort Sumter side (as will be see by the chart). There was also a narrow channel on the northern side, towards which the obstructions were constantly drifting, owing probably to the holding ground being better on that side. These obstructions are all I can hear of until those put down within the last four months, and from my informant it seems there were no others.

Those recently placed were simply a rope (6′′) one hundred feet long, with an eye in one end by which a smaller rope and anchor was attached. The largest rope had buoys attached, and swung to the tide. There were eighty of these anchored in lines one hundred feet apart. Were placed on the line A B (on chart). There were also a number of floating barrel torpedoes put down at the same time, which were to explode by concussion; but the number or position of these I have been unable to determine. The only obstructions now visible on the surface of the water are the piles in Hog and Folly Island channels.

     Respectfully submitted.
      Your obedient servant,
 (Signed)   WM. H. DENNIS,
        Asst. U. S. Coast Survey.

To Major-General Q. A. GILLMORE,
 Commanding Department of the South.

An Account of Parrott Guns expended in the operations against the Defences of Charleston, in 1863 and 1864.

The Report of the "Engineer and Artillery Operations against Charleston in 1863," contains an account of twenty-four Parrott rifles expended in service during these operations, viz.: one 30-pounder (4.2'' bore) sixteen 100-pounders (6.4'' bore), six 200-pounders (8'' bore), and one 300-pounder (10'' bore). Four of the 200-pounders, and two of the 100-pounders, gave way by breaking square off under the wrought-iron band near the vent.

The 100 and 200-pounders sustained an average of 310 rounds per gun.

One 200-pounder and seven 100-pounders gave way laterally, just in front of the band, by the blowing out of an oblong piece, which in some cases extended well back under the band, without injuring the latter, and without causing cracks or evidences of strain elsewhere.

The 300-pounder and one 100-pounder broke off at the muzzle, leaving a jagged end. In the 300-pounder the lands were chipped off to a point below the termination of the fracture. After this the piece was used again, and fired as well as before, apparently.

The other eight guns of the twenty-four broke into several fragments each, one of them (the 30-pounder) into as many as seven, and none of them into less than three.

In only four cases out of the twenty-four was the wrought-iron bands broken.

Besides the twenty-four Parrott rifles mentioned above, twenty-seven others were subsequently expended during the year 1864, while Major-General J. G. Foster had command of the Department of the South, in bombarding Charleston City and the ruins of Fort Sumter.

The history of these guns as furnished by Lieutenant-Colonel Ames, 3d R. I. Artillery, Chief of Artillery of the Department, is contained in the following table. No drawings of the bursted guns were preserved.

SUPPLEMENTARY REPORT. 35

HISTORY OF PARROTT RIFLED GUNS EXPENDED IN FORT WAGNER, BATTERY GREGG, AND BATTERY CHATFIELD (MORRIS ISLAND, S. C.) IN 1864.

Caliber.	Elevation when Burst.	Greatest Elevation used.	Total number of Rounds fired.	Number of Premature Explosions.	Weight of Gun in Pounds.	Year of Fabrication.	Foundry Number.	Foundry Initials.	Founder's Initials.	Inspector's Initials.	Number of Gun.	Charge.
(a) 100-pounder, 6.4″...	35° 00″	40° 00″	241	2	9,842	1863	487	W. P. F.	R. P. P.	A. M.	66	10 lbs. No. 7 Powder.
(b) 100-pounder, 6.4″...	35 00	35 00	1,006	7	9,802	1863	698	W. P. F.	R. P. P.	A. M.	99	10 lbs. No. 7 "
(c) 30-pounder, 4.2″...	2 45	18 00	2,900	..	4,200	1862	727	None.	None.	A. M.	..	
(d) 100-pounder, 6.4″...	31 00	35 00	1,134	..	9,804	1863	246	W. P. F.	R. P. P.	A. M.	14	10 lbs. No. 7 "
(e) 100-pounder, 6.4″...	38 00	38 00	13	1	9,777	1863	...	W. P. F.	R. P. P.	T. E.	156	10 lbs. No. 7 "

(a) BATTERY GREGG, MAY 9, 1864.—This gun had been fired one hundred and eight (108) rounds, at from 4° to 7° elevation, previous to its being mounted to shell Charleston. An oblong piece was blown off, including right half of gun and right trunnion, and extended back under reinforce six (6) inches; breech, from vent, blown out of reinforce to rear; reinforce uninjured. Distance to object fired at, 6,820 yards.

(b) BATTERY GREGG, MAY 15, 1867.—This gun had been much used in left batteries. Six (6) rounds only were fired from it at the city. A crack appeared at the sixth round fired on Charleston, extending from under front of reinforce, and in a line with the vent, to a point twelve (12) inches in front of right trunnion, and on a line with it. Distance to object fired at, 6,230 yards.

(c) BATTERY GREGG, MAY 15, 1864.—Mounted in Battery Gregg, soon after the fort came into our possession. Fired two thousand four hundred (2,400) rounds, at an elevation of 18°. Ninety-five (95) rounds fired from it since January 1, 1864. Gun proper burst in eight (8) pieces. Reinforce broken in halves longitudinally. Distance to object fired at, 1,375 yards.

(d) BATTERY GREGG, MAY 19, 1864.—One thousand one hundred (1,100) rounds had been fired from this gun previous to its being mounted to shell the city, at from 8° to 15° elevation. At the thirty-fourth round fired on Charleston it burst into eight (8) pieces, including all that portion of the gun in rear of trunnions. Reinforce broke in halves, longitudinally. Distance to object fired at, 6,820 yards.

(e) BATTERY GREGG, MAY 27, 1864.—At the thirteenth (13th) round fired from this gun upon Charleston, an oblong piece including about one-third the circumference of the gun blew out, between a point four (4) inches under reinforce (where it broke short off), and a point twenty (20) inches forward of trunnions. Distance to object fired at, 6,820 yards.

HISTORY OF PARROTT RIFLED GUNS EXPENDED IN FORT WAGNER, BATTERY GREGG, Etc.—Continued.

Calibre.	Elevation when Burst.	Greatest Elevation used.	Total Number of Rounds fired.	Number of Premature Explosions.	Weight of Gun in Pounds.	Year of Fabrication.	Foundry Number.	Foundry Initials.	Founder's Initials.	Inspector's Initials.	Number of Gun.	Charge.
(f) 100-pounder, 6.4″...	6° 15″	15° 00″	226	5	No rec'd	1863	670	W. P. F.	R. P. P.	A. M.	100	10 lbs. No. 7 powder.
(g) 30-pounder, 4.2″...	36 00	40 00	401	10	3,500	none	none	W. P. F.	R. P. P.	None.	18	3¼ lbs. Mortar pdr.
(h) 100-pounder, 6.4″...	3 15	6 30	491	21	9,728	1863	121	W. P. F.	R. P. P.	A. M.	No recd.	10 lbs. No. 7 powder.
(i) 200-pounder, 8″ ...	3 00	18 15	1,457	10	16,522	1863	754	....	....	....	20	
(j) 200-pounder, 8″ ...	3 10	3 35	578	11	16,537	1863	857	W. P. F.	....	T. E.	25	

(f) BATTERY CHATFIELD, JUNE 6, 1864.—A piece (oblong) extending to and including left trunnion, was blown off from gun. It appeared to break short off about three inches under reinforce.

(g) BATTERY GREGG, JULY 7, 1864.—This gun was a Navy size 30-pounder; sixteen (16) inches of muzzle blown off by premature explosion of shell in gun. The bore of the gun on being examined was found to be without a defect or flaw. Distance to object fired at, 6,820 yards.

(h) BATTERY CHATFIELD, JULY 15, 1864.—An oblong piece was blown out of upper half of gun. It broke short off two (2) inches under reinforce, and extended twelve inches beyond the trunnions. The upper half of trunnions scaled off.

(i) BATTERY GREGG, JULY 23, 1864.—The breach was thrown to the rear, the reinforce being slightly expanded at its rear. Two or three longitudinal cracks extend from this point along the bore toward the exterior surface of the gun, in front of the reinforce. At the seat of the shot in this gun, crevices an inch deep were found in each groove of the rifling. Prior to its being mounted in Battery Gregg, four hundred and sixty-eight (468) rounds were fired from it at 4° to 12° elevation. These rounds are comprised in the total 1,457, given in the above table.

(j) BATTERY GREGG, JULY 30, 1864.—Mounted in Battery Gregg, July 8, 1864. Of the eleven (11) premature explosions, six (6) occurred in the last two (2) days' firing. The fracture consists of a crack across the right side of the breach toward the vent, and continued on a line with and under the reinforce to the left trunnion. No pieces were thrown off. Distance to object fired at, 1,375 yards.

SUPPLEMENTARY REPORT. 37

HISTORY OF PARROTT RIFLED GUNS EXPENDED IN FORT WAGNER, BATTERY GREGG, ETC.—Continued.

Caliber.	Elevation when Burst.	Greatest Elevation used.	Total Number of Rounds fired.	Number of Premature Explosions.	Weight of Gun in Pounds.	Year of Fabrication.	Foundry Number.	Foundry Initials.	Founder's Initials.	Inspector's Initials.	Number of Gun.	Charge.
(k) 300-pounder, 10″...	4° 5″	7° 10″	1,207	5								25 lbs. Mammoth pdr.
(l) 200-pounder, 8″...	4 10	4 10	269	6	16,462	1863	962	W. P. F.	R. P. P.	T. E.	24	16 lbs. No. 5 powder.
(m) 200-pounder, 8″...	3 10	6 45	1,063	12	16,534	1863	829	W. P. F.	R. P. P.			
(n) 100-pounder, 6.4″...	31 00	36 00	1,480	..	9,797	1862	272	W. P. F.	R. P. P.	None.	23	10 lbs. No. 7 powder.
(o) 100-pounder, 6.4″...	36 00	36 40	316	1	9,727	1864	808	W. P. F.	R. P. P.	R. M. H.	187	10 lbs. No. 7 "

(k) BATTERY CHATFIELD, AUGUST 1, 1864.—Shell burst prematurely in gun, blowing off twenty-six (26) inches of muzzle. Two hundred (200) rounds had been fired from this gun previous to its being brought into this department. One thousand and seven (1,007) rounds were fired from it while in the Department of the South. Crevices half (½) an inch in depth were found in front of seat of shot.

(l) BATTERY CHATFIELD, AUGUST 5, 1864.—At two hundred and sixty-ninth (269th) round a crack appeared extending from under reinforce to left trunnion. Crack commenced on inside of bore extending through to outer surface of gun.

(m) BATTERY GREGG, AUGUST 15, 1864.—The reinforce of the gun was broken into many pieces, number not known; most of them were blown out of the battery by the explosion. Distance to object fired at, 1,375 yards.

(n) BATTERY GREGG, SEPTEMBER 4, 1864.—This gun had been used during the "Siege of Fort Wagner." The record of its firing at that time cannot be found. The grooves are all well worn. Just in front of seat of shot the iron is much corroded. Crevices from one-half (½) to one quarter (¼) of an inch in depth are found where the lands join the grooves. A slight crack appeared extending from under the reinforce toward the left trunnion. Gun was dismounted to prevent the chance of loss of life by its bursting. Distance to object fired at, 6,820 yards.

(o) BATTERY GREGG, SEPTEMBER 12, 1864.—Ninety (90) rounds were fired from this gun with a charge of ten (10) pounds; the cartridge was then increased to eleven (11) pounds. The charge was too great, as much of the powder was blown out of the gun. The shell in the gun at the time of its bursting was thrown a distance of 5,000 yards from the battery. Gun was broken into four (4) pieces. That portion within the reinforce was broken in halves. Reinforce uninjured. Distance to object fired at, 6,820 yards.

HISTORY OF PARROTT RIFLED GUNS EXPENDED IN FORT WAGNER, BATTERY GREGG, Etc.—Continued.

Calibre	Elevation when Burst.	Greatest Elevation used.	Total Number of Rounds fired.	Number of Premature Explosions.	Weight of Gun in Pounds.	Year of Fabrication.	Foundry Number.	Foundry Initials.	Founder's Initials.	Inspector's Initials.	Number of Gun.	Charge.
(p) 100-pounder, 6.4″...	35° 00″	37° 00″	31	1	9,807	1864	843	W. P. F.	R. P. P.	R. M. H.	186	11 lbs. No. 7 powder.
(q) 100-pounder, 6.4″...	29 50	29 50	705	3	9,777	1863	117	W. P. F.	R. P. P.	T. E.	162	10 lbs. No. 7 "
(r) 100-pounder, 6.4″...	35 00	35 00	883	7	9,777	1863	481	W. P. F.	R. P. P.	None.	81	10 lbs. No. 7 "
(s) 100-pounder, 6.4″...	33 00	35 00	914	..	9,779	1863	957	W. P. F.	R. P. P.	None.	128	10 lbs. No. 7 "

(p) BATTERY GREGG, SEPTEMBER 13, 1864.—Eleven (11) pounds No. 7 (Dupont's) powder was used in the cartridge of this gun, by order of Brigadier-General Saxton, notwithstanding that the bursting of last gun (o), showed conclusively that eleven pounds of powder could not be burned in the gun. Breach was blown out of reinforce, and gun was broken squarely off about one inch and a half (1½ inches) in rear of vent. A very small crack seemed to extend to the vent. Reinforce uninjured. The gun was perfect in every other respect. Distance to object fired at, 6,820 yards.

(q) BATTERY GREGG, SEPTEMBER 17, 1864.—Five hundred (500) rounds were fired from this gun, at an average elevation of 6°, and two hundred and five (205) at an elevation of 29° 50′. All that portion of the gun in rear of trunnions was blown into an innumerable number of pieces, many of which were blown out of the battery. The reinforce was broken into nine (9) pieces. The shell did not burst in the gun, but was thrown about 4,000 yards. Distance to object fired at, 6,820 yards.

(r) BATTERY GREGG, NOVEMBER 14, 1864.—This gun was obtained from the Naval Ordnance Depot, St. Helena. The upper half of the gun, from base of breach to trunnions, was blown off into many pieces. Most of them were blown out of the battery, and lost in the marsh. The reinforce was broken into four (4) pieces. At seat of charge crevices an inch in depth were found where the grooves and lands join. The shell from the gun at the time of its bursting reached the city. Distance to object fired at, 6,820 yards.

(s) BATTERY GREGG, NOVEMBER 14, 1864.—This was a navy 100-pdr. Parrott. Fracture commenced about four (4) inches under reinforce, and in a line with vent (a slight crack extending through this latter point). About one-half of gun (right half, including right trunnion) was split off; reinforce much out of shape at front. At seat of charge the iron was much corroded. Crevices were discovered at this point about one-sixteenth of an inch in depth. Five hundred (500) long shells had been fired from this gun. The shell in this gun at time of bursting reached the city. Distance to object fired at, 6,820 yards.

SUPPLEMENTARY REPORT. 39

HISTORY OF PARROTT RIFLED GUNS EXPENDED IN FORT WAGNER, BATTERY GREGG, BATTERY CHATFIELD, Etc.—Continued.

Calibre.	Elevation when Burst.	Greatest Elevation used.	Total number of Rounds fired.	Number of Premature Explosions.	Weight of Gun in Pounds.	Year of Fabrication.	Foundry Number.	Foundry Initials.	Founder's Initials.	Inspector's Initials.	Number of Gun.	Charge.
(t) 200-pounder, 8″	25° 00″	34° 00″	272	2	16,562	1864	53	W. P. F.	R. P. P.	R. M. H.	3	16 lbs. No. 7 powder.
(u) 100-pounder, 6.4″	35 00	35 00	1,225	5	9,834	1862	372	W. P. F.	R. P. P.	None.	34	10 lbs. No. 7 "
(v) 100-pounder, 6.4″	11 10	11 10	454	6	9,804	1862	242	W. P. F.	R. P. P.	None.	18	10 lbs. No. 7 "
(w) 100-pounder, 6.4″	9 10	18 00	617	7	9,757	1862	510	W. P. F.	R. P. P.	A. M.	67	10 lbs. No. 7 "
(x) 100-pounder, 6.4″	35 00	35 00	102	1	9,702	1864	908	W. P. F.	R. P. P.	R. M. H.	190	10 lbs.

(*t*) BATTERY CHATFIELD, OCTOBER 1, 1864.—At the two hundred and seventy-second (272d) round the breach was blown out of reinforce, having broken off squarely, just in front of the vent. Shell fired from gun at time of its bursting reached Charleston. Distance to object fired at, 6,930 yards.

(*u*) BATTERY GREGG, NOVEMBER 13, 1864.—Twelve (12) inches of muzzle blown off by the premature explosion of a shell in the chase of the gun. The grooves are slightly worn. At seat of charge the bore is enlarged and metal much corroded. This gun was obtained from Naval Ordnance Depot at St. Helena. Distance to object fired at, 6,280 yards.

(*v*) FORT WAGNER, NOVEMBER 15, 1864.—The fracture of this gun extended from three (3) inches under reinforce to the trunnions. The upper portion of the gun between these two points was broken into ten (10) pieces. Reinforce was some injured. Rifling of gun in perfect order, sharp, with no signs of being worn.

(*w*) FORT WAGNER, NOVEMBER 15, 1864.—At six hundred and seventeenth (617th) round the gun burst in six (6) pieces in rear of trunnions. Reinforce broken into three (3) pieces. Shell fired from gun at the time of its bursting reached the object fired at.

(*x*) BATTERY GREGG, NOVEMBER 28, 1864.—All of this gun in rear of trunnions broke into a large number of pieces. The reinforce was also broken. Two-thirds of the shell fired from this gun were long shells. Distance to object fired at, 6,820 yards.

HISTORY OF PARROTT RIFLED GUNS EXPENDED IN FORT WAGNER, BATTERY GREGG, ETC.—Continued.

Calibre.	Elevation when Burst.	Greatest Elevation used.	Total number of Rounds fired.	Number of Premature Explosions.	Weight of Gun in Pounds.	Year of Fabrication.	Foundry Number.	Foundry Initials.	Founder's Initials.	Inspector's Initials.	Number of Gun.	Charge.
(y) 100-pounder, 6.4".	35° 00''	35° 00''	196	3	9,727	1864	888	W. P. F.	R. P. P.	R. N. H.	189	10 lbs. No. 7 powder.
(z) 100-pounder, 6.4".	34 00	34 00	1,590	Unk'wn	9,760	1862	454	W. P. F.	R. P. P.	A. M.	52	10 lbs. No. 7 "

(y) BATTERY GREGG, NOVEMBER, 29, 1864.—An oblong piece was blown off left side of gun. This piece included the left trunnion, where the fracture terminated. Reinforce uninjured. Distance to object fired at, 6,820 yards.

(z) BATTERY CHATFIELD.—One thousand and two (1,002) rounds were fired from this gun at Charleston. Five hundred and eighty-eight (588) were fired at low elevation. All that portion of gun in rear of trunnions was broken into a large number of pieces. Reinforce broken in halves.

NOTE.—In the above table the column giving the "Number of Premature Explosions" is of little practical value, for it has been ascertained upon inquiry, that it contains a record, not only of the shells which burst in the bore of the gun, but, in many cases, of those that burst in front of the piece after leaving it. The record, therefore, affords no reliable means of judging to what extent, if any, the bursting of the guns is due to the bursting of the projectiles within the bore.

Q. A. G.

JOURNAL

OF THE

DEFENCE OF FORT SUMTER, ETC.

NOTE.—The following collection of telegrams, extracts from Journal, etc., sent from Fort Sumter to Confederate headquarters in Charleston, was taken from a book found with a portion of General Beauregard's baggage, captured soon after the evacuation of the city. Although they comprise much unimportant and some irrelevant matter, it has been deemed best to omit nothing contained in the book, and to preserve the order in which they were there found arranged.—Q. A. G.

Telegrams received Headquarters Department South Carolina, Georgia, and Florida, from Fort Sumter, from the date of July 9, 1863:

FORT SUMTER, July 9, 5 A. M.

Captain W. F. NANCE, *A. A. G.:*

There are twenty-eight vessels off bar, including four (4) monitors.

(Signed,)   A. RHETT,
Colonel Commanding.

FORT SUMTER, July 10, 1863, 5:18 A. M.

Captain NANCE, *A. A. G.:*

The enemy have just opened heavy fire on Mitchell.

(Signed,)   ALFRED RHETT,
Colonel Commanding.

Received at 5:45 A. M.
    (Signed,)   G. T. B.

FORT SUMTER, July 10, 6:10 A. M.

Captain NANCE, *A. A. G.:*

Mitchell is replying slowly from his guns; three monitors have crossed the bar, and are moving up to Morris Island.

(Signed,)   ALFRED RHETT,
Colonel Commanding.

SUMTER, July 10.

Captain NANCE:

Three monitors inside; the foremost has opened fire on Captain Mitchell.

     (Signed,) ALFRED RHETT,
           Colonel Commanding.

Received at 8 A. M.
 (Signed,) G. T. B.

FORT SUMTER, July 10.

Captain NANCE:

Colonel Yates telegraphs me, "batteries gone." Colonel Graham is fighting them with infantry. Let three companies of Charleston Battalion come down at once, if possible. Have a light battery with a few horses sent, if you can. Hold some infantry in reserve in town, and have some to be sent to Sullivan's Island, if required. What news from Simonton? Lieutenant Bee killed, Lieutenant Alston wounded.

     (Signed,) R. S. RIPLEY,
          Brigadier-General Commanding.

SUMTER, July 10, 1863.

Captain NANCE, *for* General JORDAN:

Our troops have been driven back to Battery Wagner. Cummings Point Battery has opened on the pursuers. Fort Sumter just opening. Monitors are shelling Battery Wagner. I do not think it well to send more troops to Morris Island immediately, as there are enough there to crowd the works we hold. Has General Hagood arrived? Should any guns arrive they had best be put in position in first White Point Battery.

     (Signed,) R. S. RIPLEY,
         Brigadier-General.

Received at 10:45 A. M.
  (Signed,) G. T. B.

FORT SUMTER, July 10, 1863, 2:30 P. M.

General THOMAS JORDAN:

Firing from Morris Island and Sumter at enemy's troops on Morris Island. Will endeavor to arrange two torpedoes.

     (Signed,) R. S. RIPLEY,
         Brigadier-General.

FORT SUMTER, July 10.

Captain W. F. NANCE, *A. A. G.*:

Lieutenant-Colonel Yates requests that engineers be sent down this evening to repair damanes.

(Signed,) ALFRED RHETT,
Colonel Commanding.

FORT SUMTER July 11, 1:35 A. M.

Brigadier-General JORDAN,
Mills House:

Have visited Battery Wagner. Its guns are all in order. Olmstead's battalion in position but troops jaded; which regret, as the enemy, I am satisfied, do not intend to hold island in force. Graham's old camps have been burned and destroyed—intelligence by a wounded man who crept through marsh. Have ordered Graham to send out a force to drive in their pickets.

(Signed,) R. S. RIPLEY,
Brigadier-General.

FORT SUMTER, July 11, 5:20 A. M.

Captain W. F. NANCE, *A. A. G.*:

Enemy assaulted Battery Wagner at daylight this morning. Have been repulsed.

(Signed,) ALFRED RHETT,
Colonel Commanding.

Received at 6:30 A. M.
(Signed,) G. T. B.

FORT SUMTER, July 11, 7:15 P. M.

Captain W. F. NANCE, *A. A. G.*:

The fifth monitor has just crossed the bar.

(Signed,) A. RHETT,
Colonel Commanding.

Received at 7:30 P. M.
(Signed,) G. T. B.

FORT SUMTER, July 12, 5 A. M.

Captain NANCE, *A. A. G.*:

No assault on Battery Wagner. I am shelling Morris Island.

(Signed,) ALFRED RHETT,
Colonel Commanding.

FORT SUMTER, July 12, 7:25.

Captain NANCE, *A. A. G.:*

There are twenty-two vessels outside and inside of bar. Five dispatch boats inside, five monitors inside. "Ironsides" in same position. Two French vessels off bar.

(Signed,)   JULIUS M. RHETT,
1st Lieutenant and Officer of Day.

FORT SUMTER, July 13.

Captain NANCE, *A. A. G.:*

Two (2) of enemy's barges out of range, apparently anchored off shoals at Pumpkin Hill channel.

(Signed,)   ALFRED RHETT,
Colonel Commanding.

Received 12:30 P. M.

FORT SUMTER, July 14, 7:25.

Captain W. F. NANCE, *A. A. G.:*

No change in the fleet since last night.

(Signed,)   E. W. PARKER.

FORT SUMTER, July 14.

Captain NANCE, *A. A. G.:*

Thirty-two vessels off the bar, including one Frenchman, four monitors, and eight steamboats.

(Signed,)   F. H. HARLESTON,
Captain and Officer of Day.

FORT SUMTER, July 15, 1863, 7:30 P. M.

Captain NANCE, *A. A. G.:*

The "Ironsides" has crossed the bar. Twelve vessels are now inside the bar, including four monitors and the "Ironsides." Fourteen (14) vessels are outside the bar, including one French vessel.

(Signed,)   D. G. FLEMING,
Captain and Officer of Day.

FORT SUMTER, July 16.

Captain W. F. NANCE, *A. A. G.:*

There are eighteen vessels inside the bar, including four monitors and the "Ironsides;" sixteen outside. Two off Maffitt's channel, four off North channel, and five off Little Folly Island.

(Signed,)   ALFRED RHETT,
Colonel Commanding.

FORT SUMTER, July 16.

Captain W. F. NANCE, *A. A. G.*:

The enemy are putting up works about three miles from here, just below Gregg's Hill.

(Signed,) ALFRED RHETT,
Colonel Commanding.

FORT SUMTER, July 16, 7:25 P. M.

Captain W. F. NANCE, *A. A. G.*:

There are thirty-six vessels in sight; thirteen outside, including a monitor and a French vessel, eighteen off Battery Wagner, and five in Folly River.

(Signed,) ALFRED RHETT,
Colonel Commanding.

FORT SUMTER, July 18.

Brigadier-General JORDAN:

Brigadier-General Taliaferro will soon be here; will order as soon as I learn situation fully from him; there are troops enough to hold now on island. Whether practicable to get more there before morning, doubtful. The enemy made three assaults, badly repulsed. One hundred prisoners, one Lieutenant-Colonel, and one Major. The dead cannot, of course, be estimated at present. Our pickets are thrown well to the Point.

(Signed,) R. S. RIPLEY,
Brigadier-General Commanding.

SUMTER, July 18.

General JORDAN:

We still hold the battery, and have been reinforced by Harrison's regiment. Pickets have been thrown far in advance, insomuch that Sumter has been requested to cease firing. General Hagood has gone over with his staff, and General Taliaferro is expected to return; more news expected soon.

(Signed,) R. S. RIPLEY,
Brigadier-General.

HEADQUARTERS FIRST REGIMENT S. C. ARTILLERY,
FORT SUMTER, July 18, 1863.

GENERAL,—I have the honor to forward the following extract from Journal kept at this post, in compliance with Special Orders No. 141, Department Headquarters:

July 17.—At 2 A. M. beat long roll, remained at battery thirty minutes, no attack, sounded recall: shifted 32-pounder rifled gun from N. W. casemate battery to Gorge battery. 6 A. M. shipped to Sullivan's Island one 10-inch sea-coast mortar and bed with two hundred and ninety-six shells. 6½ P. M.—Enemy's battery, Morris Island, fired on steamboats arriving at wharf. This is first shot from land battery in direction of fort. Fort replied by bursting four percussion shells on island. Engineer work progressing.

Preparations being made to strengthen southern wall by filling officers' quarters with cotton bales and sand. Lower casemates on western face being converted into an hospital, and advancing rapidly toward completion. Sally-port being cut on western face to enable boats to arrive under cover of fort.

At 7½ P. M. one hundred negro laborers arrived

Very respectfully, your obedient servant,

(Signed,) ALFRED RHETT,
Colonel Commanding.

FORT SUMTER, July 19, 6:35 A.M.

Brigadier-General JORDAN:

Keitt's people have not arrived. Do send the steamer over now with Graham's. Would risk her positively. Does General Beauregard order it?

(Signed,) R. S. RIPLEY.

FORT SUMTER, July 19, 6:37 A. M.

Brigadier-General JORDAN:

The "Sumter" is here with Graham's regiment, but it is broad daylight, and she cannot land within two thousand yards of the "Ironsides" and monitors. To send her over would be to trust to the enemy entirely. Shall I do it?

(Signed,) R. S. RIPLEY,
Brigadier-General.

FORT SUMTER, July 19, 6:40 A. M.

Brigadier-General THOMAS JORDAN:

Have received the following from General Hagood:

"MORRIS ISLAND, 19.

"To General RIPLEY:

"Having arrived here to-night, my knowledge of location is not "sufficient to enable me to answer your inquiry; but Lieutenant- "Colonel Harris, who was here during the bombardment, is of the

"opinion, if we had three or four thousand reliable troops here now,
"we could drive the enemy off the island. To make a move before
"daylight. Prisoners report four Brigadier-Generals in front of us,
"and fifth on Folly Island,

"(Signed,)   JOHNSON HAGOOD."

It will be impossible to get three or four thousand men over at present. Keitt and Graham have not arrived. Taliaferro has gone on to the city. Enemy's fleet off Battery Wagner, in shelling position.

(Signed,)   R. S. RIPLEY.
Brigadier-General.

FORT SUMTER, July 19, 6:45 A. M.

General THOMAS JORDAN:

Please let me know whether General Beauregard desires me to send the "Sumter" over. If the risk is to be taken, well! If not, she is wanted elsewhere for work. My own opinion is, that the work and communication must be done at night entirely. Keitt's regiment not here, and I doubt whether transportation can be furnished.

(Signed,)   R. S. RIPLEY,
Brigadier-General.

HEADQUARTERS FIRST REGIMENT S. C. ARTILLERY,
FORT SUMTER, July 19, 1863.

GENERAL,—I have the honor to forward the following extract from Journal kept at this post:

July 18.—Enemy opened this morning from two newly-constructed batteries on Morris Island, one at base of high hills on lower part of island, consisting of, apparently, eight guns, and the other on old site of Vinegar Hill, consisting of two guns and a mortar. By 11 o'clock A. M. three wooden gunboats, five monitors, and the "Ironsides" had opened on Battery Wagner. Fire exceedingly heavy; twenty-seven shells a minute bursting in and around battery. 7:20 P. M. enemy assaulted battery: after engagement of three hours and five minutes were repulsed. During day we shelled enemy's position, and expended ammunition as follows: 10-inch Columbiad shell, forty-five; 9-inch Dahlgren shell, seventeen; 8-inch Columbiad shell, thirty; 42-pounder rifle shell, three; 32-pounder bolts, eighteen; 32-pounder rifle shell, twelve; one hundred and twenty-five shot in all. Engineer work still progressing and the hospital nearly completed. Have made hastily-constructed wharf opposite sally-port. Sent, with orders to report to Captain Mitchell, commanding batteries on Shell Point, James Island, thirty men of Co. I.

    Very respectfully,
      Your obedient servant,
        (Signed,) ALFRED RHETT,
          Colonel Commanding.

          FORT SUMTER, July 20, 3 P. M.
Captain NANCE, *A. A. G.*:

General Hagood reports 10-inch gun dismounted.
      (Signed,) ALFRED RHETT,
         Colonel Commanding.

          FORT SUMTER, July 20.
Captain W. F. NANCE, *A. A. G.*:

We got her range. The "Ironsides" drew off and has ceased firing.
      (Signed,) ALFRED RHETT,
         Colonel Commanding.

      HEADQUARTERS FIRST REGIMENT S. C. ARTILLERY,
         FORT SUMTER, July 20.

GENERAL,—I have the honor to make the following extract from Journal kept at this post:

July 19, 1863.—Day comparatively quiet. Enemy sent in flag of truce. Our men engaged burying dead of both sides. Steamer "Margaret and Jessie" ran blockade safely. Several barges loaded with men came from large frigate outside at dark, and lay off position occupied by "Ironsides." Garrison slept at the guns during entire night. 8:30 A. M. fired one gun to clean the piece. Engineer works still progressing, and rooms on Gorge face being filled with cotton and sand. Most work done at night.

    Very respectfully,
      Your obedient servant,
        (Signed,) ALFRED RHETT,
          Colonel Commanding.
Brigadier-General THOMAS JORDAN,
    Chief of Staff.

         FORT SUMTER, July 21, 1863.
Captain NANCE, *A. A G.*:

Thirty vessels inside and outside the bar this evening, besides several steamers in-shore.
      (Signed,) F. H. HARLESTON,
         Captain and Officer of Day.

Captain W. F. NANCE:

Another steamboat from the fleet to Morris Island, apparently loaded with troops.

(Signed,) F. H. HARLESTON,
Captain and Officer of Day.

FORT SUMTER, July 21, 1:45 P. M.

Captain NANCE:

Two steamboats loaded with men have passed up Lighthouse Inlet. They landed on Morris Island.

(Signed,) F. H. HARLESTON,
Captain and Officer of Day.

HEADQUARTERS FIRST REGIMENT S. C. ARTILLERY,
FORT SUMTER, July 21.

GENERAL,—I have the honor to make the following extract from Journal kept at this post:

July 20, 1863, 3:30 A. M.—Steamer "Sumter" got aground five hundred yards in front of fort, but having taken off fifty men was got off.

11:20 A. M.—Enemy's batteries, fleet and land, opened on Wagner and continued fire until 6:20 A. M., when fleet ceased; mortar batteries kept up fire during entire night.

12:20 P. M.—Gunboat in creek beyond Black Island opened fire. At 2 P. M. a shell from enemy's batteries struck the fort, and continuous fire was kept up upon us till dark. One shot struck cotton bale defences on parapet and set it a fire. Drummer boy Graham severely wounded. At 3:30 P. M. Captain Mitchell's battery on Shell Point, opened fire. At 3:57 Fort Sumter opened fire on "Ironsides" and enemy's batteries. At 4:30, "Ironsides" retired.

Night quiet except enemy's mortars firing on Wagner. Seventeen shots were fired by fort at enemy during the afternoon. Engineer work progressing. New sally-port nearly completed.

Very respectfully,
Your obedient servant,
(Signed,) ALFRED RHETT,
Colonel Commanding.

Brigadier-General THOMAS JORDAN,
Chief of Staff.

FORT SUMTER, July 22, 9:10 A. M.

Captain NANCE, *A. A. G.:*

A great many tents near Lighthouse Inlet have, I think, disappeared. There are five steamboats in the inlet. Some men aboard.

    (Signed,)   ALFRED RHETT,
Colonel Commanding.

FORT SUMTER, July 22, 9:20 A. M.

Captain NANCE, *A. A. G..*

There are fifteen (15) wooden vessels, the "Ironsides" and five monitors off Morris Island, and six wooden vessels outside, making twenty-seven off the bar.

    (Signed,)   D. G. FLEMING,
Captain and Officer of Day.

HEADQUARTERS FIRST REGIMENT S. C. ARTILLERY,
FORT SUMTER, July 22.

GENERAL,—I have the honor to make the following extract from Journal kept at this post:

July 21.—Unable to dismount guns ordered to be sent away for want of proper implements. Enemy apparently mounted eight new guns on their batteries this side of Graham's house. At 11:20 A. M. enemy's land batteries and two wooden gunboats opened on Battery Wagner. This was kept up till evening. No firing took place here. New sally-port nearly completed. Wharf on western face has been floored, and is capable of bearing heavy guns. One of lower rooms on southern face has been filled with cotton and sand, and a second one about half done.

    Very respectfully,
        Your obedient servant,
            (Signed,)   ALFRED RHETT,
Colonel Commanding.

Brigadier-General THOMAS JORDAN,
    Chief of Staff.

FORT SUMTER, July 23, 1863.

Captain NANCE, *A. A. G.:*

There are thirty-one vessels in sight, twelve outside the bar, seventeen inside, and two in Folly River.

    (Signed,)   ALFRED RHETT,
Colonel Commanding.

DEFENCE OF FORT SUMTER. 51

SUMTER, July 23, 7:30 P. M.

Captain NANCE, *A. A. G.*:

There are twenty-nine vessels in sight, eight outside and twenty-one inside.

(Signed,) ALFRED RHETT,
Colonel Commanding.

HEADQUARTERS FIRST REGIMENT S. C. A.,
FORT SUMTER, July 23.

GENERAL,—I have the honor to make the following extract from Journal kept at this port:

July 22.—At 12 M. two monitors firing upon Battery Wagner, the fire irregularly kept up during the day. 5 P. M. battery near Vinegar Hill opened fire. No firing from this fort during the day. 3 P. M. one double-banded Brooke gun arrived. Engineer work pushed rapidly forward.

Very respectfully,
Your obedient servant,
ALFRED RHETT,
Colonel Commanding.

Brigadier-General THOMAS JORDAN,
Chief of Staff.

SUMTER, July 24.

Captain NANCE, *A. A. G.*:

Ten (10) vessels over the bar, nineteen wooden vessels, five monitors, and "Ironsides" inside the bar off Battery Wagner, and five river steamers inside the bar off Vinegar Hill and in Folly Inlet.

(Signed,) MCMILLAN KING,
Lieutenant and Officer of the Day.

SUMTER, July 24, 7 P. M.

Captain NANCE, *A. A. G.*:

Nineteen vessels inside the bar, five iron-clad monitors and the "Ironsides" off Battery Wagner, six river steamers inside the bar off Vinegar Hill and Little Folly Inlet. Eleven vessels over the bar, one two-masted gunboat off Big Folly.

(Signed,) MCMILLAN KING,
Lieutenant and Officer of the Day.

HEADQUARTERS FIRST REGIMENT S. C. A.,
FORT SUMTER, July 24.

GENERAL,—I have the honor to make the following extract from Journal kept at this post:

July 23.—No firing on either side. The Brooke gun was mounted during the night on southeast face. Engineer work progressing, and rooms on each side of sally-port being filled.

Very respectfully,
Your obedient servant,
(Signed,) ALFRED RHETT,
Colonel Commanding.

Brigadier-General JORDAN,
Chief of Staff.

FORT SUMTER, July 25.

Captain NANCE:

Another monitor appeared in sight a few minutes ago off Middle Channel. Is now moving in slowly. The fleet now number twenty-five inside bar, including "Ironsides," and five monitors. Four tug-boats, six supply schooners, and nine gunboats, and eleven vessels outside bar, including one monitor. Enemy replying to Shell Point battery from Craig's Hill.

(Signed,) A. S. GAILLARD,
Captain and Officer of the Day.

HEADQUARTERS FIRST REGIMENT S. C. ARTY.,
FORT SUMTER, July 25.

GENERAL,—I have the honor to make the following extract from Journal kept at this post:

July 24.—At 5:30 A. M. the enemy opened a heavy fire from five monitors, the "Ironsides," and Mortar Battery. At 9:30 A. M. firing occurred from creek running towards Black Island. The tops of both magazines have been traversed with sand-bags. The filling of lower rooms on Gorge face three-fourths completed. One 10-inch Columbiad dismounted during night from northwest face and put on wharf.

(List of shells fired during night.)

Very respectfully,
Your obedient servant,
(Signed,) ALFRED RHETT,
Colonel Commanding.

Brigadier-General THOMAS JORDAN,
Chief of Staff.

DEFENCE OF FORT SUMTER. 53

FORT SUMTER, July 26.

Captain NANCE, *A. A. G.*:

"Margaret and Jessie" passed out last night. There appeared to be no firing at her. The firing was from this fort and Captain Mitchell's battery, and was quite heavy between twelve and one this morning. All quiet in front. Do not see the Yankees working. "Ironsides" taking in ammunition or coal. Monitors have their awnings stretched.

(Signed,) ALFRED RHETT,
Colonel Commanding.

SUMTER, July 26.

Captain NANCE, *A. A. G.*:

There are eleven vessels off the bar, seventeen vessels inside including the "Ironsides," and five monitors, one having left, going South. Three gunboats, one tug, balance supply ships.

(Signed,) JULIUS M. RHETT,
Lieutenant Artillery and Officer of the Day.

HEADQUARTERS FIRST REGIMENT S. C. A.,
FORT SUMTER, July 26, 1863.

GENERAL,—I have the honor to make the following extract from Journal kept at this post, viz. :

July 25, 1863.—During the morning the enemy kept up a fire upon this fort at long intervals, from 30-pounder Parrott guns.

During the day and night we shelled the enemy's rifle-pits and lower battery. There were one hundred and four shells fired during the whole time. Five rooms on Gorge face filled with cotton and sand.

One 10-inch Columbiad, carriage and chassis, shipped during night to Sullivan's Island.

Very respectfully,
Your obedient servant,
(Signed,) ALFRED RHETT,
Colonel Commanding.

Brigadier-General THOMAS JORDAN,
Chief of Staff.

SUMTER, July 27.

Captain NANCE, *A. A. G.*:

Thirty-five vessels in sight: twenty-seven inside the bar, including "Ironsides," and five monitors. The rest steamboats and wooden

vessels, supply and monitor boats. No material change since morning.
      (Signed,)   ALFRED RHETT,
            Colonel Commanding.

      HEADQUARTERS FIRST REGIMENT S. C. A.,
        FORT SUMTER, July 27.

GENERAL,—I have the honor to make the following extract from Journal kept at this post:

July 26.—During night shelled enemy's batteries at intervals of fifteen minutes. Expended ammunition as follows: 10-inch Columbiad shell, twenty-six; 8-inch Columbiad shell, thirteen; 9-inch Dahlgren shell, four; 7-inch rifle shell, five; 32-pounder rifle shell, three. One 8-inch navy shell-gun dismounted during night and ready for shipment. Engineer work being carried on; sally-port in Gorge face, guard-room, and cells, now being filled.

   Very respectfully,
    Your obedient servant,
     (Signed,)   ALFRED RHETT,
           Colonel Commanding.
Brigadier-General THOMAS JORDAN,
   Chief of Staff.

           SUMTER, July 28.
Captain NANCE, *A. A. G.:*

Frigate "Ironsides," four monitors, about twenty-one gunboats, supply vessels, and steamboats, inside the bar. Ten vessels outside the bar.
      (Signed,)   ALFRED RHETT,
            Colonel Commanding.

         SUMTER, July 28, 10:30 A. M.
Captain NANCE, *A. A. G.:*

The enemy have opened two mortar batteries on Battery Wagner. One wooden gunboat also firing.
      (Signed,)   Colonel RHETT.

        FORT SUMTER, July 28, 7 P. M.
Captain NANCE, *A. A. G.:*

Twenty vessels inside the bar, including five monitors and "Ironsides;" twelve vessels outside the bar.
      (Signed,)   Colonel RHETT.

DEFENCE OF FORT SUMTER. 55

HEADQUARTERS FIRST REGIMENT S. C. A.,
FORT SUMTER, July 28, 1863.

GENERAL,—I have the honor to make the following extract from Journal kept at this post:

July 27.—A fire upon the enemy's upper battery was kept up during the entire night, at intervals of fifteen minutes. The following ammunition was expended: twenty 10-inch, twelve 8-inch, and twenty-eight 9-inch shell. Two 8-inch Columbiads, two carriages, and two chasses were dismounted during the night, and are on the wharf ready for shipment. Six rooms on Gorge face filled with sand; eight still to be filled.

Very respectfully,
Your obedient servant,
(Signed,) ALFRED RHETT,
Colonel Commanding.

Brigadier-General THOMAS JORDAN,
Chief of Staff.

SUMTER, July 29.

Captain NANCE:

Mortar Battery on Black Island opened apparently at Legare's Point.

(Signed,) F. H. HARLESTON,
Captain and Officer of the Day.

SUMTER, July 29.

Captain NANCE:

"Ironsides," four monitors, five gunboats, nine supply ships, and three steamboats inside. Nine vessels, including one Frenchman, outside. Several steamboats and schooners in Lighthouse Inlet.

(Signed,) F. H. HARLESTON,
Captain and Officer of the Day.

SUMTER, July 29.

Extract from Journal kept at post:

July 28.—Two 8-inch Columbiads shipped at 2 P. M. At 3 P. M. one 8-inch navy shell gun, fifty-five cwt., placed on wharf for shipment. All these guns have one hundred rounds of ammunition shipped with them. Two more 8-inch Columbiads, two chasses, and two carriages placed on wharf for shipment. The eight rooms on lower tier, Gorge face, have nearly been completed. One room on second tier was commenced at 12 M., and is now about half filled. The earth is being taken from the parade. During night kept up fire from this post at intervals of fifteen minutes. Expended ten 10-inch Columbiad shell, seven 8-inch Columbiad shell, eight 9-inch Dahlgren shell, four 7-inch rifle shell, ten 32-pounder rifle shell.

(Signed,) ALFRED RHETT,
Colonel Commanding.

SUMTER, July 30.

Captain Nance:

One monitor, one wooden gunboat, two mortars near Graham's house, and one mortar near Craig's Hill, are firing at Battery Wagner and Battery Gregg.

(Signed,) ALFRED RHETT,
Colonel Commanding.

SUMTER, July 30.

"Ironsides" has opened fire, endeavoring to shell the troops scattered among the sand-hills at the Point.

(Signed,) I. R. PRINGLE,
Lieutenant and Officer of the Day.

SUMTER, July 30.

Position of fleet the same. Four monitors and "Ironsides," and twelve vessels inside; six in rear of Little Folly.

(Signed,) I. R. PRINGLE,
Lieutenant and Officer of the Day.

SUMTER, July 30.

Extract from Journal kept at this post:

July 29.—Engineer work progressing. All lower rooms filled; now working at two of upper ones. Fired at "Ironsides" several times about 1 P. M., and during the night shelled enemy's upper battery at intervals of fifteen minutes. Expended twelve 10-inch, four 9-inch, eight 8-inch, ten 42-pounder, and nine 32-pounder shell. One 8-inch Columbiad, chassis and carriage on wharf during night, and ready for shipment.

[(Signed,) ALFRED RHETT,
Colonel Commanding.

DEFENCE OF FORT SUMTER. 57

SUMTER, July 31.

Captain NANCE:

All quiet this morning. The "Ironsides" occupies her usual position. There are four monitors and four gunboats inside. Enemy opened fire last night at three o'clock, with six monitors.

(Signed,) ALFRED RHETT,
Colonel Commanding.

SUMTER, July 31, 7:55 P. M.

At sunset the "Ironsides," four monitors, and eleven wooden vessels were inside the bar, and eight wooden vessels outside. Several schooners and steamboats in Lighthouse Inlet.

(Signed,) D. G. FLEMING,
Captain and Officer of the Day.

SUMTER, July 31.

Extract from Journal kept at this post:

July 30.—"Ironsides" moved up at 12:20 P. M. and opened fire on Battery Wagner. After repeated shots from this fort she retired at 1:15. A monitor was fired at several times between 6:30 and 7 P. M. One room on upper floor has been completed, two more being filled. One 42-pounder with carriage and chassis, and one 8-inch navy shell gun, fifty-five cwt., on wharf for shipment.

July 31, 4 A. M.—Enemy opened on Battery Wagner with six mortars; we replied at intervals of two minutes. Firing ceased about 5:30 A. M. Expended eighteen 10-inch Columbiad shell, six 8-inch Columbiad shell, three 7-inch Brooke rifle, twelve 9-inch Dahlgren, and six 32-pounder rifle shell.

(Signed,) ALFRED RHETT,
Colonel Commanding.

SUMTER, August 1, 1863.

Captain NANCE:

A large river steamer transport with troops coming from the north, and passing south, over the bar.

(Signed,) ALFRED RHETT,
Colonel Commanding.

SUMTER, August 1, 1863, 10:40 A. M.

Transport before mentioned has come inside the bar and anchored off Morris Island. Small boat communicating with the island.

(Signed,) ALFRED RHETT,
Colonel Commanding.

Thirty-five vessels in sight; eighteen outside the bar, seventeen inside, including three monitors and "Ironsides."

      (Signed,) ALFRED RHETT,
           Colonel Commanding.

       SUMTER, August 1, 1863, 7:10 P. M.

Sixteen vessels over the bar. Fourteen vessels inside the bar; nine wooden gunboats, four monitors, and "Ironsides." Several schooners and river steamers in Lighthouse Inlet.

      (Signed,) McMILLAN KING,
        Lieutenant and Officer of the Day.

         SUMTER, July 1, 1863.

Enemy's batteries at foot of Craig's Hill opened upon steamer "Chesterfield" at point of Morris Island; she was not struck.

      (Signed,) ALFRED RHETT,
           Colonel Commanding.

      SUMTER, August 1, 1863, 10:40 P. M.

Enemy opened fire on steamer "Chesterfield," at Cummings Point. Captain and mate deserted her, and the corporal of the guard and negro pilot brought her off safely to Fort Sumter. What shall I do with the boat?

      (Signed,) ALFRED RHETT,
           Colonel Commanding.

       FORT SUMTER, August 1, 1863.

Extract from Journal kept at the post:

July 31.—Seven 10-inch mortar shell were fired between 7 P. M. and 8:30 P. M. from mortar mounted on end of wharf on southern face. One 8-inch navy shell gun, sixty-three cwt., was dismounted, and is on the wharf ready for shipment. Engineer work progressing, and two rooms on second floor are filled; three more in different stages of completion.

August 1.—At 3:45 A. M. enemy again opened on Wagner from his mortars. We replied. In past twenty-four hours expended seven 10-inch mortar shell, five 10-inch Columbiad shell, and one 7-inch rifle shell.

      (Signed,) ALFRED RHETT,
           Colonel Commanding.

DEFENCE OF FORT SUMTER.

SUMTER, August 2, 7:30.

Captain NANCE, *A. A. G.:*

There are ten vessels in sight outside the bar, eighteen inside the bar, including "Ironsides," and four monitors; also eight schooners and steamboats in Lighthouse Inlet.

(Signed,)   ALFRED RHETT,
Colonel Commanding.

SUMTER, August 2, 9:40 P. M.

There are twelve vessels outside the bar, eighteen inside, and six river steamers and schooners in Lighthouse Inlet.

(Signed,)   ALFRED RHETT,
Colonel Commanding.

SUMTER, August 2.

Extract from Journal kept at post:

August 1.—The day was unusually quiet, and no firing took place from fort except from 10-inch mortar on end of wharf. Expended six 10-inch mortar shells. Two rifled 32-pounders were dismounted and taken outside the fort. The wharf proper has sunken much from the length of time that guns have been left there without being taken off. No more rooms have been started by engineer. Work progressing. At 9:05 P. M. the enemy opened fire upon steamer "Chesterfield," landing at Cummings Point. At 9:15 P. M. she got off uninjured. Just before the firing commenced a rocket was thrown up from somewhere in the marsh, and as soon as the steamer started another was fired, both evidently from a corps of observation stationed for that purpose. Captain Harleston with detachment of Company "D," who have gone to Morris Island for the past three nights to mount two 10-inch Columbiads, had to be brought over this morning in small boats at 3 A. M., August 1, the steamer being unable to go for them. The provisions for the Charleston Battery had to be carried in same manner. Very respectfully,

Your obedient servant,
(Signed,)   ALFRED RHETT,
Colonel Commanding.

SUMTER, August 3, 8 A. M.

There are thirty-seven vessels in sight, nine outside the bar and twenty-eight inside, nineteen of which are off Morris Island. The rest, nine in number, are in Lighthouse Inlet.

(Signed,)   ALFRED RHETT,
Colonel Commanding.

SUMTER, August 3, 9 A. M.

There are eighteen vessels inside of bar, besides "Ironsides" and four monitors. Eight steamers outside of bar. River steamer and a few schooners in Lighthouse Inlet.

   (Signed,) JULIUS M. RHETT,
       Lieutenant and Officer of the Day.

SUMTER, August 3, 10:20 A. M.

Fifteen vessels outside the bar, sixteen inside bar; six river steamers in Lighthouse Inlet, six schooners in Lighthouse Inlet; two barges filled with men lying near battery where steamer "Manigault" was burned. Yankees still working in marsh beyond battery named above.

   (Signed,) A. S. GAILLARD,
       Captain and Officer of the Day.

SUMTER, August 3, 1863.

Extract from Journal kept at post:

August 2, 1 P. M.—The enemy commenced rapid bombardment of Wagner from his mortars. We replied vigorously, and enemy slackened fire in about one hour. We expended two 32-pounder rifle shell, ten 7-inch rifle, thirty 10-inch Columbiad, thirteen 10-inch mortar, twelve 9-inch Dahlgren, forty 8-inch Columbiad shell. Engineer work still progressing; five rooms on upper floor filled, two in progress. Wharf sunk so much yesterday that it broke in, and it is now dangerous to carry heavy guns on it to be shipped. It is now being repaired. Captain Harleston, with detachment of Company "D," again went to Morris Island last night, and succeeded in mounting second 10-inch Columbiad. Two mechanics have been sent from this post to repair fuses at Wagner. Ammunition for Wagner had to be carried from this post last night, by a crew detailed from this garrison, with our boat.

   (Signed,) ALFRED RHETT,
       Colonel Commanding.

SUMTER, August 4, 9:30 A. M.

The enemy appears as if they had landed troops on the south point of Morris Island. New tents have just been pitched.

   (Signed,) JULIUS M. RHETT,
       Lieutenant and Officer of the Day.

SUMTER, August 4.

There has been no material change in the fleet since last report. "Ironsides" taking in ammunition. Working party are on east end of Black Island, and appear as if building a bridge or causeway to Morris Island.

(Signed,) JULIUS M. RHETT,
Lieutenant and Officer of the Day.

SUMTER, August 4, 7:30 P. M.

There are six schooners, three gunboats, four monitors, and "Ironsides" inside of bar. Nine steamers off bar including one large ocean steamer. Large three-masted steamer off Craig's Hill.

(Signed,) JULIUS M. RHETT,
Lieutenant and Officer of the Day.

SUMTER, August 4.

Extract from Journal kept at post:

August 3.—Day quiet, no firing from this post. Steamer "Sumter" was driven away from Morris Island last night. She was forced to return here without landing provisions. A crew was detailed from this garrison, and the rations and ordnance stores were carried over in barges. The signals on arrival and departure of "Sumter" at Morris Island, were signalled by the enemy with a single rocket, from apparently the position where steamer "Manigault" was burned. Engineer work still progressing, but no more rooms filled. One mortar and bed were taken down from terreplein, and is now ready for shipment.

(Signed,) ALFRED RHETT,
Colonel Commanding.

SUMTER, August 5, 9 A. M.

Twenty-one vessels inside bar, including "Ironsides" and four monitors. Thirteen vessels outside bar; four steamers and five schooners in Lighthouse Inlet.

(Signed,) Colonel RHETT.

SUMTER, August 5.

There are sixteen vessels inside of bar, "Ironsides," four monitors, three tug-boats, six schooners, two gunboats. Outside of bar ten steamers. There are also a few schooners and two or three river steamers in Folly Inlet.

(Signed,) JULIUS M. RHETT,
Lieutenant and Officer of the Day.

SUMTER, August 5, 1863.

Eighteen wooden vessels, four monitors, and "Ironsides" inside bar; ten vessels and English man-of-war outside bar; five steamers and five schooners in Lighthouse Inlet.

(Signed,)   ALFRED RHETT,
Colonel Commanding.

SUMTER, August 5, 1863.

Extract from Journal kept at post:

August 4.—No firing from this fort. A smooth bore 32-pounder which has been lying on South Wharf, was brought in to be mounted in casemate. The 10-inch mortar mounted on wharf was also brought in, to be mounted in parade. A boat's crew from this garrison was employed during the greater part of the night in transporting provisions to Morris Island. Lieutenant Alston, with detachment of fourteen men, Company "E," left during night for Wagner. Engineer work still being pushed forwards. Seven rooms on upper floor are filled. Two rooms on upper floor at south sallyport are the only ones remaining.

(Signed,)   ALFRED RHETT,
Colonel Commanding.

SUMTER, August 6.

At 7 o'clock A. M. the "Ironsides," four monitors, and thirteen wooden vessels were inside the bar; nine wooden vessels, including the British sloop-of-war, were outside. A number of schooners and steamboats in Lighthouse Inlet.

(Signed,)   D. G. FLEMING,
Captain and Officer of the Day.

SUMTER, August 6, 9:30 A. M.

Thirty-seven vessels in sight, ten outside the bar, fifteen inside the bar, including monitors and "Ironsides." Twelve in Lighthouse Inlet.

(Signed,)   JOHN MIDDLETON,
Lieutenant and Officer of the Day.

SUMTER, August 6.

Troops are being put on board a river steamer at Little Folly. Cannot make out whether they are being put on another larger vessel, or landed on Morris Island. No change in fleet.

(Signed,)   JOHN MIDDLETON,
Lieutenant and Officer of the Day.

SUMTER, August 6, 1863.

Extract from Journal kept at post:

August 5.—One 10-inch mortar was mounted in the parade, and a platform for another is nearly completed. A 42-pounder carriage and chassis (barbette) arrived. Last two rooms on upper floor are being filled with cotton and sand. Company "H" was transported to Morris Island last night, and Company "C" relieved and transported here by our own boats. Eighteen 7-inch rifle shell, and three 32-pounder rifle shell, were fired at enemy's batteries during afternoon.

(Signed,)   ALFRED RHETT,
Colonel Commanding.

SUMTER, August 7.

There are thirty-eight vessels in sight; of these thirteen are outside the bar, seventeen inside the bar, including "Ironsides" and monitors, and eight in Lighthouse Inlet.

(Signed,)   JNO. MIDDLETON,
Lieutenant and Officer of the Day.

SUMTER, August 7, 9:30 A. M.

Thirty-four vessels in sight, fourteen outside bar, twenty inside, including three monitors and "Ironsides;" three shots just fired from land battery at Gregg.

(Signed,)   EDWARD LOWNDES,
Lieutenant and Officer of the Day.

SUMTER, August 7, 4:10 P. M.

Thirty-seven vessels in sight, fourteen outside bar, and twenty-three inside, including monitors and "Ironsides."

(Signed,)   EDWARD LOWNDES,

SUMTER, August 7.

Two schooners lying off Folly Inlet laden with troops; a large steamer has just landed, on Morris Island, a large number of men from Folly Island

BOYLSTON,
Adjutant.

] SUMTER, August 7, 11:45 P. M.

Lieutenant-Colonel YATES:

Got the mortar twice to the surface of the water, fell back each time. Can't you send some one down early in the morning to help when tide is low? My men are worn out.

(Signed,) F. H. HARLESTON,

SUMTER, August 7, 1863.

Extract from Journal kept at post:

August 6.—One 24-pounder and one 10-inch mortar were dismounted from Gorge. One rifled 32-pounder removed from northeast casemate and mounted on Gorge. Rooms on upper floor will be completed in about twelve hours. The gate of new sally-port was hung to-day. Expended ten 10-inch shell, five 9-inch, four 7-inch rifle, three 32-pounder, three 10-inch Columbiad shell.

(Signed,) ALFRED RHETT,
Colonel Commanding.

SUMTER, August 8.

There are thirty-nine vessels in sight, seven outside, including a French vessel, twenty inside of Morris Island, including "Ironsides," and three monitors; twelve river steamers and schooners in Folly River.

(Signed,) ALFRED RHETT,
Colonel Commanding.

SUMTER, August 8, 7 P. M.

The enemy opened a brisk fire from their batteries this evening, and we commenced shelling them with three guns and two mortars.

(Signed,) ALFRED RHETT,
Colonel Commanding.

SUMTER, August 8, 1863.

Extract from Journal kept at post:

August 7.—Expended:—shell, ten 10-inch mortar, one 9-inch Dahlgren, one 7-inch rifle; shot, two 9-inch one 8-inch bolts, two 7-inch rifle. The second 10-inch mortar was mounted in the parade. A 24-pounder was brought from Gorge, and is now on wharf ready for shipment. Merlons have been put between guns, on eastern face. A traverse is being built at southeast angle, to protect guns on eastern face; it is already near level of parapet. Two attempts to raise 10-inch mortar which fell overboard whilst being shipped for Morris Island, were made during the night, but failed.

(Signed,) ALFRED RHETT,
Colonel Commanding.

SUMTER, August 9, 12:40

At 11 A. M. one gunboat went outside bar. There are now twelve vessels outside, and twenty-one vessels, three monitors, and "Ironsides" inside; eight vessels in Lighthouse Inlet.

(Signed,) G. E. HAYNESWORTH,
Lieutenant and Officer of the Day.

HEADQUARTERS FIRST REGIMENT S. C. A.,
FORT SUMTER, August 9, 1863.

Captain W. F. NANCE, *A. A. G.:*

CAPTAIN,—I have the honor respectfully to protest against the dismounting and shipping of the double-banded Brooke gun, mounted on the southeast angle of the fort.

I would respectfully call the attention of the Commanding General to the fact that this is the most important position, and the gun is one of the best in the fort.

I would also respectfully state, that already three 10-inch Columbiads, six 8-inch Columbiads, four 8-inch navy guns, one 42-pounder, seven 32-pounders smooth bore, two 32-pounders rifled, two 24-pounders, and five 10-inch mortars, have been dismounted and shipped from this fort.

If this is to be taken away, allow me respectfully to ask that another gun of like capacity be sent down immediately.

Very respectfully,
Your obedient servant,
(Signed,) ALFRED RHETT,
Colonel Commanding.

SUMTER, August 9, 1863.

Extract from Journal kept at post:

August 8.—Mortar firing kept up at fort all night. Expended—fifty-two 10-inch mortar shell, six 7-inch rifle shell, fourteen 8-inch Columbiad shell.

The double-banded 7-inch Brooke gun was dismounted during night, and will be ready for transportation to-day. The 10-inch mortar that fell overboard was raised and carried to Morris Island.

Two 24-pounders on wharf ready for transportation. Merlons and traverse at southeast angle being pushed rapidly forward by Engineer Department.

    (Signed,) ALFRED RHETT,
            Colonel Commanding.

        SUMTER, August 10, 7:10 A. M.

The enemy have opened on Wagner heavily with their land batteries and mortars.

    (Signed,) ALFRED RHETT.

        SUMTER, August 10.

Enemy are shelling Battery Wagner, as usual, with their mortar battery. Shelling Battery Gregg with Parrott from Craig's Hill. We have just opened with two mortars.

    (Signed,) ALFRED RHETT
            Colonel Commanding.

        SUMTER, August 10.

There are forty-one vessels in sight; seven outside, twenty-four inside, off Morris Island, including the "Ironsides," and three monitors; ten river steamers and schooners in Folly Inlet.

    (Signed,) ALFRED RHETT,
            Colonel Commanding.

       SUMTER, August 10, 8:45 P. M.

What I take to be an immense Drummond light, is shining on Morris Island. I do not understand it.

    (Signed,) ALFRED RHETT,
            Colonel Commanding.

      SUMTER, August 10, 8:50 P. M.

I now think the light is thrown upon Battery Gregg, to see the steamers coming up. It is very powerful.

    (Signed,) ALFRED RHETT,
            Colonel Commanding.

       SUMTER, August 10.

Extract from Journal kept at post:

Mortar firing all night at intervals of thirty minutes. Expended nineteen 10-inch mortar shells.

Steamboats "DeKalb," "Etiwan," "Rebel," and "Sumter" arrived about 6 P. M. loaded with sand in bags. Shipped two 24-pounders to city. Removed one 32-pounder rifle gun from northeast casemate to parapet on gorge face. Brooke gun ready for shipment. Traverse and merlons on southeast angle nearly completed. A small bomb-proof for ammunition chests also being built on southeast angle.

(Signed,)   ALFRED RHETT,
Colonel Commanding.

SUMTER August 11, 7:15, A. M.

The monitors have ceased firing, and have withdrawn. The only fire upon Wagner now is from mortar battery near Graham's Headquarters.

(Signed,)   ALFRED RHETT,
Colonel Commanding.

SUMTER, August 11, 7:20 A. M.

There are forty-six vessels in sight; eleven outside, twenty-two inside, including "Ironsides," and three monitors; thirteen river steamers and schooners in Folly Inlet.

(Signed,)   ALFRED RHETT,
Colonel Commanding.

SUMTER, August 11.

There is no material change in the position of the fleet since last report. There are twenty-four vessels inside of bar, including three monitors and "Ironsides." Eight steamers outside of bar.

(Signed,)   JULIUS M. RHETT,
Lieutenant and Officer of Day.

SUMTER, August 11, 9:55 A. M.

There are seven steamers and three schooners in Lighthouse Inlet; five gunboats, twelve transport ships, three monitors, and "Ironsides" inside, and five steamers outside bar. French man-of-war and lightship just inside of bar. Large work being thrown up on west side of Craig's Hill.

(Signed,)   JULIUS M. RHETT,
Captain and Officer of Day.

SUMTER, August 11.

Extract from Journal kept at post:

August 10.—Mortar firing from the two mortars in parade kept up all night. Expended—forty-nine mortar shell, two 32-pounder rifle shell. Double-banded Brooke gun was shipped. Brooke gun from salient angle was shifted to southeast angle. A 32-pounder rifle gun was mounted on gorge face. Engineer work being advanced as rapidly as force on hand will allow. The traverse on southeast angle has been completed, and outside of gorge is now strengthened with sand. Several steamers arrived about 9:30 P. M., on their way to Morris Island, but the enemy having a powerful Drummond light shining on the point, they returned to the city.

(Signed,)   ALFRED RHETT,
Colonel Commanding.

SUMTER, August 12, 3:15 P. M.

One transport with troops went south this morning at 10:30 o'clock, and two more, also filled with troops, went south at 12:30 o'clock, after communicating by tug-boat. Nothing suspicious in movements of enemy otherwise.

(Signed,)   A. S. GAILLARD,
Captain and Officer of the Day.

SUMTER, August 12, 7:30 P. M.

Five monitors inside the bar, two having come up this afternoon, and one nondescript,—a hulk without masts, and some arrangement on her bow—something like a derrick.

(Signed,)   A. S. GAILLARD,
Captain and Officer of the Day.

SUMTER, August 12.

Extract from Officer-of-the-Day's book:

August 11.—At 9 A. M. seven steamers in Lighthouse Inlet; also three schooners. Five gunboats, twelve transport ships, three monitors, and "Ironsides," inside bar; fifth iron-clad outside bar. 9:40 A. M.—Shot fired from Battery Gregg. 12 M.—No change in the position of fleet. 6 P. M.—The enemy's upper batteries opened fire on Battery Gregg and on Wagner. There were twenty wooden vessels inside of bar, not including three monitors and "Ironsides." Eight steamers outside of bar. 7 P. M.—Fort Sumter opened fire with guns on south face.

August 12, 3:30 A. M.—The enemy's batteries commenced returning the fire of our batteries, which had kept up their shelling all night. 6:45 A. M.—The enemy open fire from one of their upper batteries upon the fort, one of their shots hitting the steamer "Hibben," and injuring her very badly; also throwing several shot in, and doing some damage to the western quarters and bakehouse.

(Signed,) ALFRED RHETT,
Colonel Commanding.

SUMTER, August 12, 1863.

Extract from Journal kept at post:

August 11.—The third 10-inch mortar was brought during night from gorge face, and landed in the parade. Mortar-firing was kept up from 9:30 P. M. Expended thirty-four mortar shell. A traverse has been commenced on gorge face, the revetment to gorge still being pushed forward.

August 12.—The steamer "Hibben" was this morning disabled at wharf, by a 200-pounder Parrott shell; seven negroes injured, three more or less seriously. Oven in bakery has been rendered useless, and about half a bushel of bricks thrown down from arch. Three shells exploded in western barracks, injuring no one. Commissary stores have been removed to three casemates on northeast angle. A small boat has been sent to Fort Johnson to bring over fresh beef.

(Signed,) ALFRED RHETT,
Colonel Commanding.

SUMTER, August 13, 10:20 A. M.

Vessels inside bar: "Ironsides," and a hulk with a mortar on board, firing at Wagner, five monitors, nine gunboats, fourteen supply vessels, one of these apparently with a mortar also. Seventeen steamboats, schooners, etc., in Lighthouse Inlet. Number of vessels outside nine, including Frenchman and lightship.

(Signed,) F. H. HARLESTON,
Captain and Officer of Day.

SUMTER, August 13, 12 M.

Five gunboats left the fleet off Battery Wagner and went north. They are now lying just inside Overall channel, and firing at the fort; their shells, as yet, have fallen a little short. I think they are out of range of the fort.

(Signed,) F. H. HARLESTON,
Captain and Officer of Day.

FORT SUMTER, August 13, 6:45.

"Ironsides," two mortar hulks, six monitors, five gunboats, ten supply vessels inside. Steamboat towing a transport into Lighthouse

Inlet; ten steamboats, schooners, etc., in Lighthouse Inlet; one steamer from south joining the fleet inside; twelve vessels outside, including Frenchman and lightship. At 3:30 P. M. four gunboats opened at four thousand yards on this fort. 6 P. M. two guns at foot of Craig's Hill opened on the fort.

(Signed,)   F. H. HARLESTON,
Captain and Officer of Day.

FORT SUMTER, August 13, 6:45.

Four wooden gunboats came in this afternoon and threw a number of shots. One struck outside, and one shell burst under mortar bed in parade, raising the platform. The enemy have opened from two 200-pounder Parrotts this afternoon.

(Signed,)   ALFRED RHETT,
Colonel Commanding.

FORT SUMTER, August 13, 10:25 P. M.

Of the Parrott shell fired this afternoon at the fort, two struck the southwest reinforce to the magazine. The penetration of one is four feet, diameter of crater four feet three inches; of the other (a glancing shot on eastern return of same reinforce), eight feet high, five feet wide, two feet deep, coming out of top of reinforce and cracked into face of old wall.

(Signed,)   O. BLANDING,
Major.

FORT SUMTER, August 13.

Extract from Officer-of-the-Day's book:

At 10:30 A. M. forty-six vessels of all kinds to be seen as follows: One river steamer in creek in Big Folly Island, seven schooners, one brig, one steamship, five steamers in Lighthouse Inlet, one two-masted vessel (side-wheel), which appeared to be a transport, off Pumpkin Hill channel, going south, too indistinct to see satisfactorily. Inside bar, off Morris Island, were nine schooners, eight gunboats, one tug-boat, three monitors, and "Ironsides." One transport with troops came from over bar, and a little north, off Ship Channel, one lightship anchored off Overall channel. "Wabash" and six other vessels over the bar from Overall to Maffit channel.

11:15 A. M.—Enemy fired a few shots from Craig's Hill at Battery Gregg, and one 200-pounder Parrott shot at Fort Sumter, the latter falling short. Transport above mentioned going south, has disappeared.

12 M.—No change of consequence since report at 10:30 A. M.

12:30 P. M.—Two transports filled with troops, after communicating by tug-boat, proceeded south. No material change during day except arrival of two monitors and a nondescript lighter. Nothing to be seen of fleet during night. Enemy opened on the fort again in evening. Brisk firing during night.

5 A. M.—Thirty-seven vessels in sight, not including those in Lighthouse Inlet.

7:30 A. M.—River steamer and schooner in creek in Big Folly Island; seven schooners, one brig, and six steamers in Lighthouse Inlet; fourteen gunboats, five schooners, five monitors, two tug-boats, "Ironsides," and nondescript lighter off Morris Island; thirteen vessels outside the bar, including lightship. At 6:30 A. M. one river steamer went south from Lighthouse Inlet.

(Signed,) ALFRED RHETT,
Colonel Commanding.

SUMTER, August 13.

Extract from Journal kept at this post:

Aug. 12.—Mortar firing kept up all night. Expended thirty-eight 10-inch mortar shell. One 8-inch Columbiad dismounted during night from east face, to be sent to Morris Island. One 10-inch Columbiad shifted, from next to 11-inch Dahlgren, to near centre of battery on east face. Central traverse on east face is now being built; the other traverse will be built to-day. Seventeen 200-pounder Parrott shot and shell struck the fort during the entire day, six outside and eleven inside. Two men were wounded—Corporal Phillips, Co. "F," and Private Norton, Co. "C;" they have been sent to the city. One 32-pounder rifle carriage was disabled, and gun struck on muzzle, not supposed to be injured. Two traverse circles on western face have been destroyed A clear breach of three feet has been made in northwest angle by a single 200-pounder shot. One wounded negro died. The wood-piles on southern side of fort have been removed to the pits, and curtains will be constructed to protect the men from fragments of bricks.

Aug. 13.—The "Mary Frances" arrived at 6 A. M. with ammunition and stores for Morris Island and this post. The enemy fired three shot, all striking outside, one injuring parapet on gorge face.

The engineer work on outside of gorge face has to be stopped during the day, on account of the enemy's shells.

(Signed,) ALFRED RHETT,
Colonel Commanding.

SUMTER, August 14, 11:10 A. M.

Inside of bar thirty-four vessels, including "Ironsides," five monitors, two mortar schooners, and twenty-six steamers, transports, gunboats, and supply schooners. Outside bar nine vessels, including steamships, schooners, and one light boat. In Folly Island Inlet and Creek fourteen vessels, including steamers, supply schooners, and transports.

(Signed,) C. W. PARKER,
Captain and Officer of the Day.

SUMTER, August 14, 12:15 P. M.

Number of vessels same as in my former report; position changed. Two small vessels having passed outside the bar in a fog about 10:30 A. M.

(Signed,) C. W. PARKER,
Captain and Officer of the Day.

SUMTER, August 14, 7 P. M.

Inside bar twenty-seven vessels, including "Ironsides," five monitors, two mortar schooners, and nineteen gunboats, steamers, and supply schooners. Outside bar thirteen vessels, including steamers, schooners, and lightships. In Lighthouse Inlet and Folly River seventeen vessels, including steamers, transports, and supply schooners.

(Signed,) C. W. PARKER,
Captain and Officer of the Day.

SUMTER, August 14.

Extract from Officer-of-the-Day's book:

August 13.—At 9 A. M. number of vessels inside the bar, lying off Wagner, "Ironsides," a hulk with a mortar aboard, five monitors, nine gunboats, fourteen supply vessels, one of them being dismantled similarly to the hulk with mortar aboard. Sixteen steamboats, schooners, etc., in Lighthouse Inlet. Nine vessels outside, including one Frenchman and a lightship. About 10:30 A. M. five gunboats left the fleet off Battery Wagner and went north until off Overall channel, when they fired once or twice at the fort. At 3:30 P. M. the gunboats fired again at the fort, they lying about four thousand yards from it. During the day a sixth monitor joined the fleet off Battery Wagner. At 6:30 P. M. "Ironsides," two mortar hulks, six monitors, ten supply vessels inside. A steamboat towing a transport south, apparently to Lighthouse Inlet. Eleven vessels outside, including Frenchman and lightship. At 6 P. M. the enemy opened fire from two guns from their batteries at the foot of Craig's Hill, upon the fort. The enemy's land batteries opened on Battery Wagner at about midnight, and continued firing during the night.

August 14.—At 7 A. M. "Ironsides," six monitors, seven gunboats, two hulks, and fourteen supply vessels, including steamboats, schooners and barges, etc., inside. Eighteen steamboats, etc., in Lighthouse Inlet. Ten vessels outside, including Frenchman, lightship, and one transport going north; no troops to be seen on board.

(Signed,) ORMSBY BLANDING,
Major Commanding.

SUMTER, August 14.

Extract from Journal kept at post:

Aug. 13.—Mortar firing all night. Expended twenty-eight 10-inch mortar shell. One 8-inch Columbiad carriage and chassis ready for shipment. The 32-pounder rifle gun which was struck and cracked. It was dismounted. The one to the right of it was shifted in its place. Four gunboats came up during the day and threw several shots at fort; one came in, burst beneath platform of one of the mortars, and temporarily disabled it. Ten shots struck fort during day, injuring no one; greatest penetration four feet. Second and third traverses, east face, nearly completed. Revetment to gorge face still being carried on.

Aug. 14.—Two shots struck fort this morning. A schooner laden with sand dragged anchor during night and was wrecked near northeast face of fort. The two men on board were saved. A shot this morning carried away top of flagstaff near southeast angle of fort.

(Signed,) ORMSBY BLANDING,
Major Commanding.

SUMTER, August 15.

Twenty-five vessels inside the bar, including six monitors and "Ironsides." Fifteen wooden vessels outside bar, and a number of schooners and steamboats in Lighthouse Inlet.

(Signed,) D. G. FLEMING,
Captain and Officer of the Day.

SUMTER, August 15.

Twenty-one wooden vessels, six monitors, and the "Ironsides" inside bar. Eleven wooden vessels outside, and a number of schooners and steamboats in Lighthouse Inlet.

(Signed,)   D. G. FLEMING,
Captain and Officer of the Day.

SUMTER, August 15, 6:55 P. M.

The enemy only fired two shots at us to-day; both passed over.

(Signed,)   ALFRED RHETT,
Colonel Commanding.

SUMTER, August 15.

Extract from Officer-of-the-Day's book:

August 14.—At 9 o'clock A. M. inside of bar thirty-four vessels, viz., "Ironsides," five monitors, two mortar boats, eight wooden gunboats, and eighteen steamers, transports, and supply schooners. Outside of bar nine vessels, viz., six steamboats, two schooners, and one lightship. Lighthouse Inlet fourteen vessels, steamers, transports, and supply schooners. 9:30 A. M. mortar boat opened on Wagner. 10:30 A. M. gunboat opened on Sumter. 11:20 A. M. Wagner opened on gunboat. 11:25 another mortar boat opened on Wagner. 12 M. number of vessels same. Two vessels passed outside while the horizon was hazy. 5 P. M. inside of bar thirty vessels, viz., "Ironsides," five monitors, two mortar boats, twenty-two steamers, gunboats, and supply schooners. 5:30 P. M. enemy opened on the fort from Craig's Hill, ceased at 6:15 P. M. 6:40 P. M. enemy opened fire on Wagner; responded to by Wagner and Gregg. 7 P. M. inside bar "Ironsides," five monitors, two mortars boats, besides nineteen vessels. Outside, thirteen. Lighthouse Inlet seventeen. 5 A. M. inside same as above. Outside sixteen. Lighthouse Inlet seventeen, class of vessels being the same. 7 A. M. same as at 5 A. M.

(Signed,)   ORMSBY BLANDING,
Major Commanding.

SUMTER, August 15.

Extract from Journal kept at post:

Firing all night (August 14th) from one mortar. Mortar platform which was disabled has been repaired, but was finished so late that we could not obtain the direction. Expended thirty-five 10-inch mortar shell. The 10-inch Columbiad next to salient was dismounted during night to be shifted to salient. A force of four hundred and seventy laborers and mechanics has been engaged in relief, day and night, upon the defences of fort. Two sand traverses on east face have been completed, and arches of western magazine covered over. The crib work on east face is being taken away, to construct blindages for shelter under gorge wall, on interior of fort. During the night three thousand sandbags were received, and two thousand five hundred were built up on exterior of gorge. The fort was struck five times from land batteries, and once by shell from gunboats. Assistant engineers White and Mikell reported for duty during the night.

(Signed,)   ORMSBY BLANDING,
Major Commanding.

SUMTER, August 16.

Enemy opened fire at four o'clock P. M. from his two most advanced batteries of Parrott guns on Fort Sumter, and ceased about seven o'clock P. M., throwing twenty-nine shots in all, with the following effect:

Struck the wall, eight; passed over, five; fell short, ten; fell within, two; struck parapet, four.

(Signed,)   A. J. HARTLEY,
Captain and Assistant Artillery Officer

SUMTER, August 16.

There are fifty-two vessels in sight—twenty-seven, including "Ironsides" and six monitors, inside bar off Morris Island; eleven vessels outside, and fourteen river steamers and schooners in Folly Inlet.

(Signed,)   ALFRED RHETT,
Colonel Commanding.

SUMTER, August 16, 8 P. M.

Forty-eight shot fired this afternoon. Four passed over, four or five fell short, ten struck inside, and ten struck outside. Two shot struck parapet above terreplein. One passed through—the other a bulging shot. The pintle of one 24-pounder has been loosened by a shot on outside below terreplein.

(Signed,)   ALFRED RHETT,
Colonel Commanding.

SUMTER, August 16.

Extract from Journal kept at post:

August 15.—Mortars in the parade were fired all through the night. Expended thirty-seven 10-inch mortar shell. The 10-inch

Columbiad was mounted during night on salient. One 10-inch mortar and bed, and one 8-inch Columbiad carriage and chassis, ready for shipment. Two shots were fired at fort from enemy's land batteries in the afternoon, both passed over. Force employed by engineers for past twenty-four hours, 450. The filling of arches over western magazine is completed. The erecting of blindage shelter, under inside of gorge face, is being carried on. 2,928 bags of sand were built up on outside of gorge, to a level with top of second story windows, in a two-bag thickness. To-night it will be up to top of parapet on western half. To the east of caponiere no work has yet been done.

    (Signed,) Alfred Rhett.
          Colonel Commanding.

        Sumter, August 17, 7:30 a. m.

The enemy have opened with a 200-pounder from this side of Graham's house, and another gun, I suppose a 100-pounder. From two 200-pounders under the hill also. They have hammered the fort a good deal, and the trunnion of a rifled 32-pounder has been knocked off. The "Ironsides" and two monitors are backing in.

    (Signed,) Alfred Rhett,
          Colonel Commanding.

       Sumter, August 17, 12:50 p. m.

Do send Wragg down. Dr. Moore is sick. We have stopped firing. The "Ironsides" and monitors have drawn off. The upper batteries have slackened fire. Six hundred and twelve (612) shots and shell have struck and passed over us. One man, "Co. F," slightly wounded since last report. All the guns except one 8-inch and one 10-inch gun on northwest front disabled.

    (Signed,) Alfred Rhett,
          Colonel Commanding.

         Sumter, Aug. 17.

I am about to open fire on iron-clad.
    (Signed,) A. Rhett.

         Sumter, August 17.

Two monitors and "Ironsides" this side of buoy; foremost opened fire on fort with rifled gun.

    (Signed,) A. Rhett,
          Colonel Commanding.

DEFENCE OF FORT SUMTER.

SUMTER, August 17.

The "Ironsides," six monitors, and six wooden gunboats, are now engaged. 9:25 A. M.—A 42 pounder on northwest battery dismounted.

(Signed,) A. RHETT,
Colonel Commanding.

SUMTER, August 17.

One more 42-pounder dismounted. Traverse circle to Gates 8-inch Columbiad shot away. Lieutenant Johnson, engineer, flesh wound in left arm below elbow. Quartermaster Sergeant Nichol, three fingers left hand cut off. Dr. Moore is sick; send medical assistance.

(Signed,) A. RHETT,
Colonel Commanding.

SUMTER, August 17.

About fifty shot and shell have come into the fort. Over one hundred have struck the walls outside. One man killed, one seriously wounded, nine slightly. Julius Rhett and John Middleton slightly bruised by bricks. Can't say what is the damage to the wall just now. The left Columbiad in Captain Harleston's battery—northeast battery—disabled. Upright shot away; 32-pounder rifled, on gorge, trunnion shot away.

(Signed,) ALFRED RHETT,
Colonel Commanding.

SUMTER, August 17, 10:45.

Up to this time four hundred and eighty shots have been fired, pounding away heavily, inside and out. No more casualties since last report.

(Signed,) ALFRED RHETT,
Colonel Commanding.

SUMTER, August 17, 11 A. M.

Nine hundred and nineteen shots have been fired, four hundred and fifty-five struck outside, two hundred and eighteen inside, two hundred and sixty-six passed over. Casualties—Barringer, Co. "K," killed; Lieutenants Rhett, John Middleton, and John Johnson, engineer, slightly wounded; Corporal Charles, Co. "C," severely wounded; Quartermaster Sergeant Nichol, four fingers cut from left hand, also twelve privates slightly wounded. The enemy are still firing once in fifteen minutes to prevent working. Mr. Johnson will endeavor, however, to fix the western magazine. The damage done to gorge face since the General was here is considerable. Engineers will report, and I will forward reports. All the guns on northwest face have been disabled, except one 8-inch Columbiad and one 42-pounder, including the big 10-inch Columbiad.

(Signed,) ALFRED RHETT,
Colonel Commanding.

SUMTER, August 18.

August 17.—At 5 A. M. seven of the enemy's guns from Morris Island opened on Sumter, five of the guns were 200-pounders in battery near Craig's Hill; at the same time fire was opened on Wagner and Gregg by the "Ironsides" and monitors, which continued until 10:45, when they engaged Fort Sumter. Sumter commenced replying at 11:15, and at 1:30 the enemy withdrew.

From 5 A. M., August 17, to 5 A. M., August 18, nine hundred and forty-eight shot and shell were fired, four hundred and forty-five of which struck outside, two hundred and twenty-three inside, and two hundred and seventy passed over. The western magazine has been traversed to a thickness of ten feet, and in height equal to first story. The second floor of eastern magazine has been covered with four feet of sand, and the same floor of the western with eighteen inches. One 32-pounder had trunnions shot away on northwest face, two 10-inch Columbiads, one 9-inch Dahlgren, one 8-inch Columbiad, and two 42-pounders were disabled; the two latter guns were taken to the parade to be shipped. The casualties for the day were one killed and seventeen wounded.

(Signed,) ALFRED RHETT,
Colonel Commanding.

SUMTER, August 18, 6:40.

There has been no material change in the fleet with the exception that the "Ironsides" has moved up nearer the fleet; the monitors are lying in line-of-battle out of range of Battery Wagner. The enemy still firing at the fort.

(Signed,) JULIUS M. RHETT,
Lieutenant and Officer of the Day.

SUMTER, August 18, 8:45 A. M.

There are thirty vessels inside of bar, including two mortar boats, six monitors, and "Ironsides;" six steamers outside, besides a great many

DEFENCE OF FORT SUMTER.

schooners in Lighthouse Inlet. "Ironsides" and two monitors, besides batteries at foot of Craig's Hill, and one below Graham's house, firing upon Fort Sumter and Battery Wagner; Battery Wagner replying slowly.

(Signed,) JULIUS M. RHETT,
Lieutenant and Officer of the Day.

SUMTER, August 18, 10:30 A. M.

Enemy have fired a good many shell this morning, with an idea, I think, of blowing out loose masonry.

(Signed,) ALFRED RHETT,
Colonel Commanding.

SUMTER, August 18, 10:20 A. M.

It is impossible to get out a gun to-day. The sally-port and the way to it is covered with rubbish, and shells continually bursting near. Two 42-pounders were taken off parapet last night, but could not be got out on the wharf.

(Signed,) ALFRED RHETT,
Colonel Commanding.

SUMTER, August 18, 1863, 11:25 A. M.

It is simply impossible to dismount or remove one disabled gun to-day.

(Signed,) ALFRED RHETT,
Colonel Commanding.

SUMTER, August 18, 1:30 P. M.

There has been no change in the position of things since my last report. "Ironsides" and two monitors have ceased firing, only land batteries continue. Have just observed a battery thrown up west of steamer "Manigault," and between it and Black Island in marsh; two guns observed at present.*

(Signed,) JULIUS M. RHETT,
Lieutenant and Officer of the Day.

SUMTER, August 18, 3:45 P. M.

The fire of the enemy's land batteries is still very heavy. The wall on the northwest face is bulged out, from the fire in reverse, in half a dozen places. The gorge wall is pretty well hammered;

---

* The marsh battery, known as the "Swamp Angel," is doubtless referred to here. It never contained more than one gun.—Q. A. G.

the greatest damage about my old room. In second casemate to the east of the sally-port, on the western face, a crack has extended through the wall from the parapet to within three feet of the berm. Am framing door through the casemates on southwest.

(Signed,)   ALFRED RHETT,
Colonel Commanding.

SUMTER, August 18, 7:50 P. M.

This afternoon five monitors and the "Ironsides" took up position in line; have been firing into the northwest front of the fort in reverse all day; every gun on that face is unserviceable. The two 10-inch Columbiads in Captain Harleston's battery are also disabled. Should the enemy contemplate moving in to-night, on the northwest face we could not open a gun. The northwest face is now in a very shattered condition.

(Signed,)   ALFRED RHETT,
Colonel Commanding.

SUMTER, August 18, 9 P. M.

The enemy again opened fire heavily at daylight. All the guns on gorge have been disabled, except two 32-pounders rifled, and one 24-pounder. Both guns on west face have been disabled. All the guns on northwest face unserviceable. Two 10-inch guns, Captain Harleston's battery, disabled. Brooke gun, southwest angle, carriage disabled. The enemy ceased fire at about 7 P. M. Seven hundred and eighty-five shell have been fired—three hundred and eighty-eight outside, two hundred and seventeen inside, one hundred and eighty-nine over. Casualties: Stewart, cockswain, seriously, arm; N. F. Devereaux, engineer corps, slightly; Corporal Bennett, Company "B," slightly. The wall of northwest face I think more seriously damaged, perhaps, than gorge wall. The gorge wall seriously damaged, will probably be breached to-morrow.

(Signed,)   ALFRED RHETT,
Colonel Commanding.

SUMTER, August 19, 6:30 P. M.

There has been no material change in the position of the fleet since my last report. There are the same number of vessels, including two mortar boats, six monitors, and "Ironsides" inside; six steamers outside. The enemy's batteries commenced firing at 4:30 A. M. this morning.

(Signed)   JULIUS M. RHETT,
Lieutenant and Officer of Day.

SUMTER, August 19, 8:40 A. M.

The enemy are working, with a large force, on a little marsh battery near Black Island.

    (Signed,) O. BLANDING,
           Major Commanding.

SUMTER, August 19, 9:12 A. M.

"Ironsides," six monitors, twelve gunboats, two mortar vessels, and fourteen supply vessels inside. So hazy can only see one or two outside. Several vessels in Lighthouse Inlet. Enemy firing from their land batteries.

    (Signed,) F. H. HARLESTON,
          Captain and Officer of Day.

SUMTER, August 19, 10:50.

At 10:20 A. M. the first shot passed through the gorge, coming out of the room on the right of the old adjutant's office. The room is known as General Ripley's room. The shot struck close under the arch where there is little sand.

    (Signed,) A. RHETT,
          Colonel Commanding.

SUMTER, August 19, 12:10 P. M.

The width of twenty feet of the gorge wall has fallen, and two-thirds will probably be down to-morrow, and light is showing through three or four of the casemates of gorge wall. One mortar dismounted and bed torn and broken. Seven casemates on west face are shattered, three pieces* shot away, and three more shattered on second tier. The same for first tier. A good part of terreplein has fallen in. One killed and four wounded. Seven hundred and sixty-two shots to-day; three hundred and ninety-eight struck outside, two hundred and thirty-six inside, and one hundred and twenty-eight over.

    (Signed,) ALFRED RHETT,
          Colonel Commanding.

SUMTER, August 19, 6:45 P. M.

Colonel Rhett sent up the colors, manned the batteries, fired two long range. I had Moultrie and other batteries in readiness, and the fleet is going out. The despatch intercepted was, "The Admiral is going to try Sumter, and wants a brisk fire kept up until he gets in:—To Colonel T. from General G." The fire is brisk, but he don't ap-

---

* Piers?

pear to be coming in. I think the demonstration has sent them off for the time, but have ordered batteries to be in readiness. Let Whitney be on hand if I don't get up, should anybody pass.

(Signed,) R. S. RIPLEY,
Brigadier-General.

SUMTER, August 19, 7:05 P. M.

A part of the gorge wall has fallen in.

(Signed,) A. RHETT,
Colonel Commanding.

SUMTER, August 19, 9:50

We need all the garrison we have to hold the fort, and are short of officers. The firing this morning is the heaviest, and the walls are seriously damaged. One killed and four wounded this morning. All gorge guns useless. Middleton went to town last night.

(Signed,) A. RHETT,
Colonel Commanding.

SUMTER, August 19, 12 M.

The "Sumter" slipped her ropes and left the wharf with one hundred and ninety barrels of powder aboard. Will try and ship the remainder by "Etiwan" this evening, if possible.

(Signed,) A. RHETT,
Colonel Commanding.

SUMTER, August 19, 12:35 P. M.

Colonel R. informs me of your wish to protect 3-gun battery. Am anxious to do it, but defer it. Will to-morrow night do? Have hospital to secure and breaches to fill.

(Signed,) JNO. JOHNSON,
Engineer.

SUMTER, August 19, 1863.

Extract from Journal kept at post:

"Ironsides" moved up, and we opened upon her at long range, firing four shots. The fire of the enemy slackened during the heat of the day, but increased in rapidity towards the afternoon, until 7 P. M., when the fire was reduced to one shot in thirty minutes. Seven hundred and eighty shots were fired, of which four hundred and eight struck outside, two hundred and forty-one inside, and one hundred and thirty-one passed over.

About one-half of the gorge wall has fallen, exposing the arches and sand in rooms. The sand-bag traverses protecting the lower rooms west of the sally-port, and a large part of the remaining gorge wall, will fall shortly. Three of the casemates were opened through sand.

On northwest face, seven casemates in the upper and lower tier are badly shattered, several of them being clean breaches, and almost all of the piers sustaining the terreplein have fallen in, and more are continually going.

Magazine still reported safe. The 10-inch mortar in parade is dismounted, and bed broken and shattered. Two of the rooms on east side of sally-port have been repacked with sand. No casualties after 9 A. M.

(Signed,) ALFRED RHETT,
Colonel Commanding.

SUMTER, August 20, 3 A. M.

I have shipped by steamers "Sumter" and "Etiwan" 35,000 pounds of powder, between three hundred and four hundred 32-pounder rifle shells, besides 7-inch projectiles, etc.

(Signed,) ALFRED RHETT,
Colonel Commanding.

SUMTER, August 20, 8:30 A. M.

"Ironsides," six monitors, two mortar boats, seven gunboats, sixteen supply vessels inside. Eight vessels outside. Eighteen steamboats, schooners, etc., in Lighthouse Inlet.

(Signed,) F. H. HARLESTON.
Captain, etc.

SUMTER, August 20, 9 A. M.

Inside bar thirty-three vessels, including "Ironsides," six monitors, six gunboats, two mortar boats, and nineteen steamers, transports, and schooners. Outside bar eight vessels, including one frigate and seven steamers, transports, and sailing vessels. In Lighthouse Inlet thirteen vessels, including steamers, transports, and sailing vessels.

(Signed,) C. W. PARKER,
Captain and Officer of the Day.

SUMTER, August 20, 12:40 P. M.

If I send out two companies, "F" and "K," it will leave but two hundred men for duty, out of these to be taken magazine men, police, cooks, old guard and new guard. I do not think it would be advisable to send volunteers amongst our garrison at this time; think it would have a bad effect. Co. "K" has been ordered to hold itself in readiness to move this evening. The firing this morning has been exceedingly heavy, more destructive than ever. Our flag has just been shot away and replaced.

(Signed,)   ALFRED RHETT,
Colonel Commanding.

SUMTER, August 20, 3:05 P. M.

I have the honor to report that at one o'clock to-day, Lieutenant Johnson of the Engineer Corps scaled the walls of Fort Sumter from the wharf, thus having the honor of being the first man in the breach.

(Signed,)   ALFRED RHETT,
Colonel Commanding.

SUMTER, August 20, 7:10 P. M.

Inside bar twenty-seven vessels, including "Ironsides," six monitors, two mortar boats, five gunboats, and thirteen steamers, transports, and supply vessels. Outside bar nine vessels, including one frigate, six steamers, transports, and supply vessels. [In Lighthouse Inlet nine vessels, including steamers, transports, and supply boats.

(Signed,)   C. W. PARKER,
Captain and Officer of the Day.

SUMTER, August 20.

Extract from Journal kept at post:

The enemy kept up to-day on Fort Sumter a heavy and continuous fire, increasing perceptibly towards the afternoon. Eight hundred and seventy-nine projectiles were thrown; four hundred and eight struck outside, two hundred and ninety-six inside, and one hundred and seventy-five over. The greater portion of the gorge wall has fallen, the debris from the upper revetting, in a manner, the lower rooms. The northwest terreplein has also, in a great degree, fallen in, and the wall has been breached in several places. Some large holes have been made in the northwest scarp wall by reverse firing to-day; six upper and three lower embrasures shattered. East scarp wall damaged very slightly. Southeast pan-coupé battered under traverse, and one-half of the parapet in its front has fallen. East magazine reinforce stone work slightly damaged, and now covered by rubbish from upper part, which is half gone.

DEFENCE OF FORT SUMTER. 85

The worst effect to-day is, that some seven feet of arch and rampart for length of thirty feet, along east half of gorge, have deen demolished. The following engineer work was done at Sumter, viz.: Hospital traverse completed, strengthened revetment to west magazine, threw over traverse from gorge wall, started traverse in rear of 3-gun battery, and packed four rooms east of gorge with sand.

One heavy 10-inch Columbiad on east face, and one rifled 42-pounder northeast face, were disabled. The flagstaff is also disabled, and flag twice shot away during the day. Nine thousand pounds of powder, and quantities of shot and shell, implements, etc., one hundred and twenty barrels pork, and seventy-five barrels flour were shipped from the fort.

One negro died from disease of the heart. Captain Gaillard and Private Donnelly, Co. "K," slightly wounded.

(Signed,)   ALFRED RHETT,
Colonel Commanding.

SUMTER, August 21, 7:40 A. M.

The enemy are enfilading our east face this morning. One heavy 10-inch, and a rifle 32-pounder in Harleston's Battery, are disabled. I expect both batteries will go to-day.

(Signed,)   ALFRED RHETT,
Colonel Commanding.

SUMTER, August 21, 9:45 A. M.

Nine vessels outside bar, twenty-six inside, and a number of schooners and transports in Lighthouse Inlet.

(Signed,)   D. G. FLEMING,
Captain and Officer of the Day.

SUMTER, August 21, 10:55 A. M.

The fire of the enemy is very heavy on the East Battery, and should the fleet come in I don't think the men could stay at the guns. Our flag has been twice shot away this morning.

(Signed,)   ALFRED RHETT,
Colonel Commanding.

SUMTER, August 21, 11:45 A. M.

We have now only nine effective guns en barbette, and the probabilities are that this afternoon most of these will be disabled.

(Signed,)   A. RHETT,
Colonel Commanding.

86   JOURNAL.

SUMTER, August 21, 2 P.M.

At 12 o'clock eleven vessels were outside the bar, twenty-seven inside, including "Ironsides," six monitors, two mortar boats. In Lighthouse Inlet fifteen schooners and steamboats.

(Signed,)   D. G. FLEMING,
Captain and Officer of the Day.

SUMTER, August 21, 7:15 P. M.

At sunset eleven vessels were outside bar, twenty-eight inside; number of schooners and steamboats in Lighthouse Inlet. All of the same character as previously reported.

(Signed,)   D. G. FLEMING,
Captain and Officer of the Day.

SUMTER, August 21, 1863, 8:45 P. M.

The firing ceased at 7 P. M. It has been very heavy all day, since 5 A. M. Nine hundred and twenty-three shots were fired. Four hundred and forty-five struck outside, two hundred and fifty-nine inside, two hundred and nineteen passed over. The eastern face has been pretty well battered. One 10-inch Columbiad, and — 8-inch Columbiads east face, and two rifled 42-pounders northeast face, were disabled; seven serviceable guns are now on parapet.

Private Thomas Powers, Co. "B," wounded severely, leg amputated above knee. Privates H. Robinson and William Dumphries, Co. "H," slightly. Corporal O'Neill and Private Goggins, Co. "K," slightly. Two negroes, Daniel, slave of Mr. Purvis, and Isaac, slave of Mr. Marmins, dangerously wounded. Flagstaff shot down four times.

(Signed,)   ALFRED RHETT,
Colonel Commanding.

SUMTER, August 21, 9:30 P. M.

The battery in marsh near Black Island appears to be built of sand, and is probably a sand battery. The fire this afternoon was the heaviest that has yet taken place. Eight hundred and seventy-nine shots were fired to-day; four hundred and twenty-eight outside, two hundred and seventy-six inside, one hundred and seventy-five over. The gorge face has been much battered, and the greater portion of it has fallen; the lower rooms, however, are in a manner revetted by the debris from the upper. The northwest wall has been breached clearly in several places, and one casemate, second floor, is entirely knocked through. Large portions of templer have also fallen. The rifle 42-pounder, Captain Harleston's battery, has been disabled. Captain Gaillard is slightly, though painfully, wounded by shell. Captain Fleming was struck, though not hurt, by a shell. Private Connelly, Co. "K," slightly.

(Signed,) ALFRED RHETT,
Colonel Commanding.

August 21, 1863.

Extract from Journal at Fort Sumter :

Lieutenant Johnson, engineer at Sumter, reports the effects of the enemy's fire to-day on the fort as follows :

"Some large holes opened through northwest scarp by reverse firing. Six upper and three lower embrasures shattered. One opening eight by ten feet. East scarp damaged very slightly. Southeast pan-coupé battered under traverse, and one-half of parapet in its front fallen. Slight damage to east magazine reinforce stone work."*

(Signed,) ALFRED RHETT,
Colonel Commanding.

SUMTER, August 22, 7:15 A. M.

Twenty-three vessels inside the bar, including six monitors, and the "Ironsides." Fourteen vessels outside bar; a number of transports in Lighthouse Inlet. The enemy opened fire on the fort at 5:30 A. M.

(Signed,) D. G. FLEMING,
Captain and Officer of the Day.

SUMTER, August 22, 8:30 A. M.

No fire can be seen from here.

(Signed,) A. RHETT,
Colonel Commanding.

SUMTER, August 22, 8:45 A. M.

Our Brooke gun is unserviceable, and can't be remounted.

(Signed,) ALFRED RHETT,
Colonel Commanding.

SUMTER, August 22, 12:15 P. M.

Thirteen vessels outside bar, thirty inside, including "Ironsides" and six monitors. "Ironsides" firing upon Batteries Wagner and

---

* This extract is from the Journal of August 20.—Q. A. G.

Gregg. Enemy's land batteries playing entirely on Sumter. Several transports in Lighthouse Inlet.

(Signed,) McMillan King,
Lieutenant Artillery and Officer of the Day.

Sumter, August 22, 1:45 p. m.

All Captain Harleston's guns have been struck, leaving us on the parapet four serviceable guns, viz.: one 11-inch and three 10-inch.

(Signed,) Alfred Rhett,
Colonel Commanding.

Sumter, August 22, 6:40 p. m.

We have but two guns en barbette serviceable.

(Signed,) A. Rhett,
Colonel Commanding.

Sumter, August 22, 6:20 p. m.

The "Ironsides" is somewhat further out on a line with point of Morris Island. You sent me a cotton-screw last night for a jackscrew; it was returned on the boat.

(Signed,) Alfred Rhett,
Colonel Commanding.

Sumter, August 22, 8:45 p. m.

Six hundred and four shots to-day. Two hundred and three struck outside, two hundred and sixteen inside, one hundred and eighty-five missed. Five arches and terreplein, northwest face, fallen in. East face much scaled by slant fire. Large craters under traverses, principal injury at level of arches and terreplein. Magazine safe. East parapet much loosened and undermined. All the barbette guns but two on the whole fort disabled, viz.: one 11-inch Dahlgren and one 10-inch Columbiad near crater of East Battery. Private Farrell, Company ' I," slightly wounded.

(Signed,) Alfred Rhett,
Colonel Commanding.

Sumter, August 22.

Brooke gun and a rifle 42-pounder, Captain Harleston's battery, this morning disabled.

(Signed,) A. Rhett,
Colonel Commanding.

DEFENCE OF FORT SUMTER.

SUMTER, August 22.

Extract from Journal kept at post:

Record of shots fired at Fort Sumter from August 16 to August 23, 1863, (both inclusive.)*

DATE.	STRUCK OUTSIDE.	STRUCK INSIDE.	MISSED.	TOTAL.	REMARKS.
August 16......	30	10	8	48	No record of projectiles fired was kept prior to the 16th inst. The first 200-pounder shots were fired on the morning of the 12th inst.
" 17......	445	233	270	948	
" 18......	452	244	180	876	
" 19......	408	241	131	780	
" 20......	408	296	175	879	
" 21......	445	259	219	923	
" 22......	203	216	185	604	
" 23......	309	225	158	692	
	2,700	1,724	1,336	5,750	

(Signed,)   A. RHETT,
Colonel Commanding.

SUMTER, August 23, 9 A. M.

Twenty-three vessels inside, including "Ironsides," monitors, gun-boats, etc.; so grouped together can't distinguish the number of each kind. Thirteen vessels outside.

(Signed,)   F. H. HARLESTON
Captain and Officer of Day.

SUMTER, August 23, 2:30 P. M.

Whilst at dinner table a shell burst just above our messroom, parts of shell coming through on the dinner table and throwing down brick. Lieutenant Boylston was seriously bruised; Lieutenant Scanlan slightly in the arm; Captain Fleming bruised; Lieutenant Ficklin slightly hurt; myself slightly hurt.

(Signed,)   ALFRED RHETT,
Colonel Commanding.

SUMTER, August 23, 6:30 P.M.

Another monitor attack to-night would imminently endanger both the parapet and west magazine, and also the relief of the garrison. To remain until to-morrow night with the hope of relieving them, would be hazardous.

(Signed,)   ALFRED RHETT,
Colonel Commanding.

---

* Col. Rhett's tabular statement comprised the number of shots fired from Aug. 16 to Aug. 22. It has been modified to include the shots fired Aug. 23.

SUMTER, August 23, 9 P. M.

Land batteries commenced firing at 7:15 o'clock A. M.; fired six hundred and thirty-three shots; ceased firing at sunset. Scaling effect on east wall and southeast pan-coupé very great. East parapet very much shattered. All guns in three-gun battery—second tier of casemates—disabled. I consider only one gun on east barbette as serviceable. One man killed to-day. One private wounded. Three negroe wounded. Three officers wounded—Lieuts. Boylston, Ficklin, and Scanlan.

(Signed,) ALFRED RHETT,
Colonel Commanding.

SUMTER, August 23, 1868.

Extract of Journal at post:

The enemy's land batteries directed their fire against Fort Sumter all day, and from 3:15 A. M. to 5:30 A. M. the monitors also engaged the fort, firing on line of east pan-coupé and west magazine. One piece of shell penetrated into ordnance store. No material damage done to magazine. Two 15-inch shell made breaches in east parapet.

The monitors threw fifty-nine shot and shell, of which twenty-seven struck outside, fifteen inside, and seventeen missed. Land batteries threw six hundred and thirty-three shots—two hundred and eighty-two striking outside, two hundred and ten inside, and one hundred and forty-one missing. Another attempt was made to hurl the 10-inch Columbiad off northwest pan-coupé during the night. Traverse over rifle 42-pounder was raised two feet higher, and northeast traverse strengthened.

The gang of negroes was relieved by others. Two hundred 8-inch shell were shipped.

(Signed,) ALFRED RHETT,
Colonel Commanding.

SUMTER, August 23, 1863.

The monitors engaged fort 3:15 A. M. to 5:30 A. M., firing on line of east pan-coupé, etc.

* * * * * *

No damage of consequence done by any of them. Fog stopped the firing half an hour ago. Sullivan's Island and Battery Simkins opened. Monitors fired thirty to forty times.

(Signed,) JNO. JOHNSON,
Lieutenant Engineers.

SUMTER, August 24, 9:55 A. M.

There are seventeen vessels inside of bar, including "Ironsides," four monitors, and twelve wooden vessels. Firing going on between Battery Wagner and enemy's lower battery, and an occasional shot at Fort Sumter.

  (Signed,)   JULIUS M. RHETT,
       Lieutenant and Officer of Day.

SUMTER, August 24.

There are twenty-four vessels inside of bar, including "Ironsides," five monitors, and the rest wooden vessels. Firing continuing between the enemy's battery and ours.

  (Signed,)   JULIUS M. RHETT,
       Lieutenant and Officer of Day.

SUMTER, August 24, 1863.

Extract from Journal kept at post:

During the day our batteries more or less engaged those of the enemy. At 9 A. M. there were seventeen vessels off bar, including "Ironsides" and four monitors; one hundred and fifty shot and shell fired at fort to-day; one hundred and twelve struck outside, fourteen inside, and twenty-four missed; one 11-inch Dahlgren, east face, the only gun serviceable. Fire of enemy to-day principally on southeast pan-coupé, and east scarp. The former had its lower casemates and embrasures breached; the latter a large displacement along its entire length, with one or two penetrations in lower casemates. During the night working parties were employed filling, with sand bags, four penetrations at lower embrasures on southeast pan-coupé and east scarp, also strengthening west magazine and repairing traverses on east barbette. 11,000 lbs. powder removed from east to west magazine. No casualties to-day in the fort.

  (Signed,)   ALFRED RHETT,
       Colonel Commanding.

SUMTER, August 25, 10:45.

Inside bar twenty-four vessels, including "Ironsides," five monitors, and eighteen gunboats and other vessels. Outside, fourteen vessels of all kinds. Ten vessels of all kinds in Lighthouse Inlet; atmosphere very hazy.

  (Signed,)   C. W. PARKER,
       Captain and Officer of Day,

SUMTER, August 25, 12 M.

Inside bar twenty-eight vessels, including "Ironsides," five monitors, two mortar boats, and twenty gunboats, steamers, transports, supply vessels, and tugs. Outside, twelve wooden vessels of all kinds. Fourteen vessels of all kinds in Lighthouse Inlet.

(Signed,)   C. W. PARKER,
Captain and Officer of Day.

SUMTER, August 25, 1863, 7:05 P.M.

* There is an assault on Battery Wagner being made at this time.

(Signed,)   A. RHETT,
Colonel Commanding.

SUMTER, August 26.

Inside bar thirty-five vessels, including "Ironsides," five monitors, two mortar boats, twenty-seven gunboats, transports, steamers, and supply vessels and tugs. Outside of bar nine vessels, including frigate, steamers, transports, and schooners. Lighthouse Inlet thirteen vessels, including steamers, transports, and supply vessels.

(Signed,)   E. S. FICKLING,
Lieutenant and Officer of the Day.

SUMTER, August 26.

Firing to-day mostly from their extreme left. Three guns at foot of Craig's Hill, one gun near Graham's house.

(Signed,)   ALFRED RHETT,
Colonel Commanding.

SUMTER, August 26.

No great increase of damage outside or inside the fort to-day. One hundred and thirty shots fired. No casualties.

(Signed,)   A. RHETT,
Colonel Commanding.

SUMTER, August 26, 6:45 P. M.

* There appears to be a heavy assault on Wagner.

(Signed,)   A. RHETT,
Colonel Commanding.

---

* There was no assault on Fort Wagner on the 25th or 26th. An attempt was made on the 25th to dislodge the enemy from a ridge, held by them between our advanced trenches and Wagner, which failed. (See Major Brooks' Journal, pp. 214 and 215.) *Another attempt succeeded on the 26th. (See pp. 216 and 217.)*

DEFENCE OF FORT SUMTER. 93

SUMTER, August 26.

Extract from Officer-of-Day's Book:

* * * * * * *

9:40 A. M.—Towards the east end of Black Island, concealed, a new battery reported unmasked by enemy, and a new buoy set, as is supposed by the enemy, at the end of shoals east of fort.

* * * * * * *

At 3:35 P. M. a shell from enemy's battery exploded on west face of brick traverse, and exploded the ammunition chest of the 11-inch Dahlgren, and three or four shell. 5:30 P. M.—Left rifle 42-pounder in northeast barbette, was dismounted and thrown backwards into parade.

* * * * * * *

(Signed,)   ALFRED RHETT,
Colonel Commanding.

SUMTER, August 26.

Extract from Journal kept at post:

August 25.—One hundred and seventy-five shot and shell fired at fort to-day. Sixty-two struck outside, thirty-six inside, seventy-seven missed. Fire to-day more destructive inside than out. Northeast casemates more or less damaged by reverse fire. East magazines uninjured. The shock of the 10-inch Parrott shell is very great. Engineer work in interior rapidly proceeded. 12,000 pounds of powder, five boxes of port fire, 7,200 priming tubes, one box paper fuzes assorted, fifty Brooke's bolts, fifty 10-inch solid shot, fifty 10-inch shell, twenty rifle shell, about fifty damaged muskets, sponges, rammers, and iron handspikes shipped on steamer "Spaulding." Cos. " C " and " F " left fort last night for duty with Lieutenant-Colonel Yates, at Fort Johnson. They were replaced by one hundred and fifty men, of two reserve regiments, of Colquitt's Brigade, under command of Captain G. W. Warthen. No casualties. Land batteries commenced firing at 6 A. M., firing slowly.

(Signed,)   A. RHETT,
Colonel Commanding.

SUMTER, August 27, 9:50 A. M.

Inside bar twenty vessels, including "Ironsides," five monitors, two mortar boats, twelve gunboats, and other vessels. Outside bar three vessels; can't make out any more on account of fog.

(Signed,)   E. S. FICKLING,
Lieutenant and Officer of the Day.

SUMTER, August 27.

Inside bar twenty vessels, including "Ironsides," and others which could not be distinguished on account of the weather. Outside bar seven vessels only can be distinguished. Some firing among pickets on Morris Island.

(Signed,)   G. W. WARTHEN,
Captain and Officer of the Day.

SUMTER, August 27, 8 P. M.

No firing to-day, with exception of four shots at flag.

(Signed,)   ALFRED RHETT,
Colonel Commanding.

SUMTER, August 27, 1863.

Extract from Journal kept at post:

August 26.—The entire day one hundred and thirty shot and shell were fired at fort. Forty-five struck outside, forty-five inside, and forty missed. Fire to-day slack and inaccurate, damage not very perceptible. Most of the holes stopped on the outside are undisturbed, and but one or two new ones made on east scarp, southeast pan-coupé and east magazine. * * * A large quantity of 10-inch mortar shells was shipped during night. Garrison at work all night. No casualties to-day. Embrasures to casemates being bricked up.

(Signed,)   A. RHETT,
Colonel Commanding.

SUMTER, August 28.

Inside bar twenty-four vessels, including "Ironsides," five monitors, two mortar and supply vessels. Outside bar eleven vessels, including frigates, steamers, transports, etc. In Lighthouse Inlet thirteen vessels, including transports and steamers.

(Signed,)   ALFRED RHETT,
Colonel Commanding.

SUMTER, August 28, 9:30 A. M.

Inside bar thirty vessels, including "Ironsides," five monitors, and two mortar boats. Outside bar ten vessels. Inlet seventeen. All quiet.

(Signed,)   J. JONES,
Lieutenant and Officer of the Day.

SUMTER, August 28.

Extract from Journal kept at post:

August 27.— * * * Working parties finished heavy traverse over 42-pounder rifle gun, East Barbette battery; repaired others on same. Discharged steamer "Etiwan," bringing five hundred bags of sand from Sullivan's Island.

About four hundred 10-inch shot and shell, one parapet gin, one lot sabots, tin straps, brass fuzes, blocks, one box bridge sights, six boxes 9-inch Dahlgren shell, one 9-inch Dahlgren gun, one lot axles-wheels, etc., for Columbiad carriage, one lot of elevating screws, were shipped at 4:30 A. M. by steamer "Etiwan."

The 9-inch Dahlgren mentioned above, and 10-inch Columbiad on northwest pan-coupé, thrown over the parapet during the night by Mr. Fraser Mathews. Completed bricking up of casemates-embrasures, lower tier. Garrison at work all day and night. No casualties.

(Signed,) ALFRED RHETT,
Colonel Commanding.

SUMTER, August 29.

There are this morning, in sight within the bar, thirty-two vessels, including "Ironsides," five monitors, and twenty-six vessels, tug-boats, supply ships, and steamers; nine vessels outside bar, and a large number of different classes of vessels in Folly Inlet. Firing from Battery Simkins.

(Signed,) JULIUS M. RHETT,
Lieutenant and Officer of the Day.

SUMTER, August 29, 1863.

Extract from Journal kept at post:

August 28.—The entire day six shots were fired; three struck outside and three missed.

No increase of damage to works.

Working parties during night completed traverse on parade at entrance to magazine and hospital, southwest angle; also repairs and improvements to East Barbette battery.

By steamer "Etiwan" were shipped the following ordnance stores:

Four hundred 10-inch mortar shell, fifteen hundred paper fuzes, one box of taps of brass fuze plugs, three damaged muskets, two elevating screws, six boxes mortar fuzes, eighteen 8-inch Columbiad incendiary shells, three 9-inch Dahlgren shells prepared, three hundred pounds lead, one 10-inch Columbiad, one sponge, eight boxes canister, one box implements, fuze extractors, etc., fragments of gin-legs, one box of fuze plugs.

Mr. Fraser Mathews threw the 9-inch Dahlgren on southwest face over the parapet; disabled in fall. Garrison worked day and night; no casualties.

(Signed,) ALFRED RHETT,
Colonel Commanding.

SUMTER, August 30, 9 A. M.

Twenty-one vessels inside the bar, including "Ironsides" and five monitors. There are seven large vessels outside bar, and a large number of supply vessels in Lighthouse Inlet.

(Signed,) ALFRED RHETT,
Colonel Commanding.

SUMTER August 30, 10 A. M.

Enemy opened upon us this morning at 6:15 o'clock with four guns. Sergeant Shaffer and two privates have been wounded.

(Signed,) ALFRED RHETT,
Colonel Commanding.

SUMTER, August 30.

Two 10-inch guns on east face have been disabled by fire to-day. I will throw them off as soon as it is dark. The only gun now left is the 11-inch gun.

(Signed,) ALFRED RHETT,
Colonel Commanding.

SUMTER, August 30.

An occasional shot from Moultrie. No change of importance to note in fleet. Enemy from Morris Island continue to shell the fort with rapidity.

(Signed,) A. RHETT,
Colonel Commanding.

SUMTER, August 30, 6:30 P. M.

The fleet is quiet; no change since 12 M. The fire on the fort did not abate in the least until 5 P. M. Since then but few shots have been fired.

(Signed,) W. P. EDWARDS,
Captain and Officer of Day.

SUMTER, August 30.

The enemy opened fire to day at 6:15 A. M. Damage to fort very great. One 10-inch Columbiad muzzle shot off, and two disabled, leaving one gun en barbette serviceable; 11-inch Dahlgren gun on parapet badly shattered; traverse badly cut up; three breaches on east face exposing sand fully. Three arches on rampart on southeast face fallen in on casemate containing commissary stores; one shot penetrated through the gorge wall; Sergeant Shaffer and three men wounded.

(Signed,)   A. RHETT,
Colonel Commanding.

SUMTER, August 30.

Extract from Journal kept at post:

August 29.—There was no firing to-day; Company "D" left for Charleston, and a detachment of the Twenty-seventh Georgia Volunteers, fifty men, under Captain Bussy, arrived here. There are ready for shipment four hundred 10-inch mortar shell, ammunition chests, wheels, etc. One Brooke gun and one 42-pounder rifled were thrown over rampart. Former shipped last night; garrison worked all day. August 30.—Fring began at 5 A. M. very rapidly; casualties, Sergeant Shaffer, Company "H," Private Laguire, Company "B," First S. C. A., Private Vau, Company "A," Twenty-seventh Georgia, slightly. Working parties engaged on second tier passage, traverse at west magazine, filling messroom, and protecting from reverse fire of monitors; also filling hole on gorge, and aiding to dismount guns. An hour was lost by separating and sending away sixty-one hands; present force one hundred and ten.

(Signed,)   A. RHETT,
Colonel Commanding.

SUMTER, August 31.

Twenty-three vessels inside the bar, including "Ironsides" and four monitors; a large number of supply vessels and steamers in Inlet; six vessels outside bar. At half-past two o'clock this morning steamer "Sumter," while coming from Morris Island with troops aboard, was fired into by batteries on Sullivan's Island, sinking the steamer and killing and wounding a number of men; also a number among those who endeavored to escape by swimming were drowned. Boats were sent as soon as possible from Fort Sumter and the gunboats, which succeeded in saving about six hundred men, who are now in the fort.

(Signed,) W. P. EDWARDS,
Captain and Officer of Day.

SUMTER, August 31.

Four monitors in line of battle coming in; two close in, and will probably open fire in a few moments.

(Signed,) ALFRED RHETT,
Colonel Commanding.

SUMTER, August 31.

The monitors have only fired a few shots at Moultrie. One monitor was thought to be fairly hit on the deck by a shot from Moultrie; no shot fired at us.

(Signed,) ALFRED RHETT,
Colonel Commanding.

SUMTER, August 31, 12 M.

I have the honor to report no change in any of the vessels inside bar. Two monitors nearer than usual to the fort, between Moultrie and Gregg, both of which are firing on them, but apparently with no effect. No firing on the fort since 10 o'clock A. M.

(Signed,) H. BUSSEY,
Captain and Officer of Day.

SUMTER, August 31.

Extract from Journal kept at post:

August 30.—The entire day six hundred and thirty-four shot and shell were fired at this post; three hundred and twenty-two struck outside, one hundred and sixty-eight inside, one hundred and forty-four missed. Shipped by steamer "Etiwan" large amount of ordnance stores. Garrison worked part of night. Casualties: Privates A. E. Woolright, Company "C," 28th Ga. Vols., and F. Ward, Company "C," 28th Ga. Vols. Damage to fort most apparent inside. On East Barbette battery two 10-inch Columbiads, serviceable up to to-day, had carriages broken; one 10-inch Columbiad muzzle shot off and dismounted. Parapet all shaky, and partially demolished; traverse badly cut up; three arches with ramparts on northeast front cut away and tumbled in, burying some commissary stores; east scarp near southeast pan-coupé has large blocks knocked away from face of second tier of casemate arches, exposing segment of arch; one hundred men at work last night; repaired traverse on either side 11-inch gun; two 10-inch Columbiads thrown over rampart.

August 31, 2:30 A. M.—Fort Moultrie fired on steamer "Sumter" by mistake; sent out barges forthwith from fort and gunboats, and saved six hundred officers and men, 20th S. C. V., and 23d Ga. Vols.

    (Signed,) A. RHETT,
           Colonel Commanding.

          SUMTER, September 1, 1863.

Extract from Journal kept at post:

August 31.—The entire day fifty-six shot and shell were fired at the fort; thirty-four struck outside, five inside, and seventeen missed. Night force engaged in securing upper west magazine passage, and casemate arches over hospital.

20th S. C. Vols., 23d Ga. Vols., and Captain Mathews' Co. Art'y left for Sullivan's Island by "Chesterfield," at 8 P. M. No casualties.

    (Signed,) A. RHETT,
           Colonel Commanding.

          SUMTER, September 1, 1863.

Extract from Officer-of-Day's book:

   *   *   *   *

6 P. M.—Four monitors came up at 3:30 P. M., evidently on a tour of observation, and after engaging Moultrie for one hour, retired. They fired a few shots at the wreck of the "Sumter." An occasional shot fired at fort since 3 P. M. until 5 P. M.

7 A. M.—Enemy opened fire on fort at 6:15 A. M.

    (Signed,) A. RHETT,
           Colonel Commanding.

        SUMTER, September 1, 12:40 A. M.

I have got the men under cover all night.

    (Signed,) A. RHETT,
           Colonel Commanding.

       SUMTER, September 1, 1:30 o'clock.

12 M.—Inside bar thirty-one vessels, including "Ironsides," six monitors, two mortar boats, and other vessels. Outside bar eleven vessels, steamers, transports, and supply vessels. Lighthouse Inlet

thirteen vessels, including steamers, transports, etc. Fire on the fort regular and destructive.

(Signed,) G. W. WARTHEN,
Captain and Officer of Day.

SUMTER, September 1, 2 P. M.

The entire terreplein on the northeast face, except the two casemates having commissary stores, have fallen in; two shots have gone into the commissary stores.

(Signed,) ALFRED RHETT,
Colonel Commanding.

SUMTER, September 1, 6 P. M.

No change observed in the fleet since noon; only large sailboat seen going southeast. The fire of the enemy from their land batteries has been incessant, and is still kept up to this hour.

(Signed,) G. W. WARTHEN,
Captain and Officer of Day.

SUMTER, September 1.

The effect of fire to-day very heavy. Three hundred and sixty-one shot fired, one hundred and sixty-six outside, seventy-five inside, one hundred and twenty over. Two shells struck in commissary stores, on the southeast face of the outside wall. Pan-coupé and next two arches have fallen. The rest of the wall is badly scaled, and in all probability will come down to-morrow as low as the first tier of casemates. We have not a gun en barbette that can be fired. Only one gun in casemate.

(Signed,) A. RHETT,
Colonel Commanding.

SUMTER, September 1.

Five monitors are coming in.

(Signed,) ALFRED RHETT,
Colonel Commanding.

SUMTER, September 2, 7:45 A.M.

Inside the bar twenty-three vessels, including "Ironsides," three monitors, two mortar boats, and others. Think there are more monitors inside bar, but they are behind other vessels; I counted at one time this morning seven. Outside bar eleven vessels, including all kinds. In Folly Inlet thirteen vessels of different sizes, and there is some object near, called a "Yankee Devil," out on a sand bank between here and Battery Wagner.

(Signed,) G. W. WARTHEN,
Captain and Officer of Day.

SUMTER, September 2, 9:40 o'clock.

There are now thirteen vessels outside bar; twenty-seven inside, including "Ironsides" and five monitors. A number of transports in Lighthouse Inlet.

(Signed,) D. G. FLEMING,
Captain and Officer of Day.

SUMTER, September 2, 12 M.

The monitors are laying off, firing steadily at Fort Sumter.

(Signed,) A. RHETT,
Colonel Commanding.

SUMTER, September 2, 1:30 P. M.

"Ironsides" coming in.

(Signed,) A. RHETT,
Colonel Commanding.

SUMTER, September 2, 6 P. M.

Nine vessels outside bar; thirty inside, including "Ironsides," five monitors, two mortar boats, and other wooden vessels. A number of transports in Lighthouse Inlet.

(Signed,) D. G. FLEMING,
Captain and Officer of Day.

SUMTER, September 2.

Extract from Officer-of-Day's book:

* * * * *

At 11:40 P. M. six monitors moved up. Fort Moultrie engaged them very rapidly at first. At 12:30 A. M. the "Ironsides" moved up and took part with monitors in firing at Sumter. At 4:40 A. M. enemy retired, the "Ironsides" first.

* * * * *

(Signed,) A. RHETT,
Colonel Commanding.

SUMTER, September 2.

Extract from Journal kept at post:

September 1.—The entire day, three hundred and eighty-two shot and shell fired at fort. One hundred and sixty-six struck outside, ninety-five inside, one hundred and twenty-one missed.

At 11:40 P. M. six monitors and the "Ironsides" moved up and commenced shelling the fort. One hundred and eighty-five shot were fired until 5 o'clock A. M. One hundred and sixteen struck outside, thirty-five inside, thirty-four over. * * Ordnance stores shipped by "Etiwan." * * * Damage very great by day and night fire. On northeast face, entire terreplein has fallen in except next northeast pan-coupé. Two shells burst in commissary stores. * * * Since monitor fire last night, every casemate, upper and lower, has been more or less breached, in most of them exposing sand bags. Three shells exploded in immediate proximity to western magazine, two so near to outer door of lower magazine passage, that, had the door been open, most serious consequences would have ensued. The third struck and brought up in sand bag traverse at passage into hospital magazine; would otherwise have gone into hospital passage used for guard-room. Slightly wounded: Privates Foshee, Colonel Rhett's Orderly, Brown, Company "C," and Alexander, Company "H," 27th Georgia Volunteers.

(Signed,)   A. RHETT,
Colonel Commanding.

SUMTER, September 3, 7 A. M.

Eight vessels now outside bar; thirty-one inside, including six monitors, the "Ironsides," and wooden vessels. Seventeen in Lighthouse Inlet.

(Signed,)   D. G. FLEMING,
Captain and Officer of the Day.

SUMTER, September 3, 11:10 A. M.

Thirty-five vessels inside bar, including "Ironsides," six monitors, and three mortar boats. Twenty-six gunboats and transports, and seven steamers outside bar. Large number in Lighthouse Inlet. No firing going on between our batteries and the enemy's.

(Signed,)   JULIUS M. RHETT,
Lieutenant and Officer of the Day.

SUMTER, September 3.

Extract from Journal at post:

September 2.—Thirty-eight shots fired at fort this day. Twelve struck outside, nine inside, and seventeen missed.

* * * * *

No material damage. One shot penetrated scarp wall, opening daylight into magazine in southeast pan-coupé. Negroes worked all day repairing previous damage, and strengthening west magazine * * * Garrison worked all day. Casemates on east face filled with sand bags. Lieutenant John Johnson, Engineer Officer, was relieved from duty at this post on account of aggravated condition of wound, and Lieutenant Hall, Engineer Officer, reported for duty in his stead. Mr. Wm. Mathews was also sent down to assist the latter. Mr. Frazer Mathews came last night for the purpose of taking off guns from berm, but in consequence of roughness of water was unable to do any work.

(Signed,) ALFRED RHETT,
Colonel Commanding.

SUMTER, September 4.

There are twenty-six vessels inside the bar, including "Ironsides" and three monitors. Six large vessels outside bar. Large number of vessels in Little Folly Inlet, consisting of steamers and supply vessels. No firing on fort this morning,

(Signed,) W. P. EDWARDS,
Captain and Officer of the Day.

SUMTER, September 4, 1863.

Report relative to condition of fort:

September 3.— * * Engineers were engaged in preparing bombproofs, and in opening embrasures in second tier of casemates, for the purpose of throwing out two 42-pounder rifled guns. During the night the 11-inch gun and the 32-pounder rifle gun were thrown over the parapet without injury, both guns having been previously disabled. There is now not a single gun en barbette; and there is but one (smooth-bore 32-pounder next the sally-port on western face) that can be fired. Mr. F. Mathews, assisted by an officer and men of the Confederate States Navy, have done good service in removing disabled guns from the fort, having dismounted and removed one 10-inch gun, and one 9-inch Dahlgren; he has also removed from the berm of the fort the Brooke gun, another 10-inch, an 8-inch, and one 32-pounder rifled gun. Lieutenant Rhett, with Company "B," has dismounted the Brooke gun, two 10-inch, one 8-inch, one 42-pounder rifled, the 11-inch, and one 32-pounder rifled gun, in the last fortnight. The northeast and northwest terrepleins have fallen in. The western wall has a crack in it, extending entirely through from parapet to berm. The greater portion of southern wall is down; the upper eastern magazine is penetrated; the lower eastern magazine wall is cracked. The east wall is very nearly shot away; a large portion of the wall is down, the ramparts gone, and nearly every casemate breached, and the remaining wall very thin. The casemates, however, on eastern face are filled with sand, sufficient to protect the garrison from shells.

I consider it impossible to either mount or use guns on any part of the parapet; and I deem the fort in its present condition unserviceable for offensive purposes. What the Engineers may effect by rebuilding or remodelling, I am unable to say. Lot of ordnance stores shipped by "Etiwan" last night. Lieutenant Grimball, Company "E," assigned to ordnance duty, has rendered efficient service in the collection and shipping of ordnance stores. Captain J. T. Champneys' Engineer Corps has reported for duty at this post. Major-General Gilmer and Lieutenant-Colonel Harris visited the fort about half-past eleven o'clock last night. Brigadier-General Ripley also came over about ten o'clock this morning. The enemy opened fire from battery on Black Island last evening.

(Signed,)   ALFRED RHETT,
Colonel Commanding.

Statement of Captain Champneys of the Engineers.

SUMTER, September 3.—I came over in the Engineers' boat with Major-General Gilmer and Colonel Starns, who, dropping me at Fort Sumter, proceeded to Cummings Point, and to Battery Wagner. I presented my orders to, and relieved Captain Gregone of the Engineers, who returned to headquarters the same night. Previous to his departure I accompanied him and Mr. Hall, Assistant Engineer, over the fort, visited the work done, and received orders from him as to its further completion. General Gilmer and Colonel Harris returning, I accompanied them over the ground and received instructions.

The hands having worked during the day, nothing was done upon the work to-night. No firing from the enemy during this night.

September 4.—I detailed twenty hands for night work, relieving them from day duty. The entire force consisted of sixty-five, with one overseer, Mr. Hyers.

Forty-five I continued at work, and finished the traverse in front of arch No. 1, in the second tier, and began to fill in arch No. 1, first tier, and secure the timber sent for the purpose of erecting splinter proofs. No firing from the enemy during the day.

Night of 4th.—Major Stephen Elliott relieved Colonel Rhett in command of the fort. The Charleston Battalion, Major Julius Blake commanding, arrived, relieving the volunteers here on duty. Sand and sand bags were to-night removed from the parapet, to fill in the arch before mentioned. No firing from the enemy to-night. Seventy-six hands with Mr. Reed, overseer, reported at 1 A. M.

September 5.—I continued all hands but fifty (whom I detailed for duty at night) to bring sand from the parapet, work which could not be done by day, upon arches 1, 2, and 3, and hauled in the timber for splinter proofs, a necessity existing for their immediate removal.

I also, at the order of Major Elliott, commanding, attended to the police duty, incumbent from the occupation of the negroes.

A few shots fired at Battery Gregg, ricocheted over the fort, but there was no immediate firing at it. Le Page, overseer, who had been absent on sick leave, reported yesterday.

Night of 5th.—I began the work of filling in the arches, with fifty men, but at 12 o'clock I turned out the entire force in order to hasten the work to completion, the difficulty of obtaining sand rendering its progress somewhat slower than I had anticipated.

I drove stakes into the floor of the hospital, and put up braces against the shutters of the embrasure windows to prevent entrance in case of assault.

Mr. William Matthews assisting me, was to-night taken down with fever. The overseer, Le Roy, reported sick.

A furious bombardment against Batteries Wagner and Gregg was kept up all day by the land batteries of the enemy and by the "Ironsides."

To-night mortar shells were thrown into Wagner, and two monitors are firing grape and shell into the channel between this fort and Sullivan Island and Morris Island. The rate of fire is one in five minutes. Some of the shot strike the fort.

I find great scarcity of lamps and oil and wick, much needed for night work.

  (Signed,)   J. T. CHAMPNEYS,
         Captain Engineers in charge.

FORT SUMTER, September 6, 1863.

Reports and Telegrams from Major Elliott, commanding Fort Sumter.

(Major Elliott relieved Colonel Alfred Rhett in the command of Fort Sumter on the night of the 4th September, 1863 ;)

September 5, 1863.

I assumed command of this post yesterday, pursuant to orders from Department Headquarters. There has been no direct fire upon the fort. Two monitors took position after dark and kept up a continuous fire upon the entrance to the harbor during the night, throwing grape and shrapnell. At about 12 15 A. M. heavy firing from the enemy's land batteries, and heavy musketry firing, induced a belief that an assault was being made upon Battery Gregg. I submit the Engineer's report, and would recommend that the timber for bomb-proofs be sawed up in the city, as there are no facilities for doing it here.

There are eighteen days' rations for the present garrison. I would also draw your attention to the fact that there is no Quartermaster at the post.

SUMTER, September 6, 10:35 A. M.

Musketry firing was reported about eleven o'clock, in the direction of the wreck of the steamer "Manigault."

September 6, 10 P. M.—Most of the wounded have been brought from Morris Island. Everything is going on right.

September 6, 11:59 P. M.—Our boats are working briskly. The enemy does not suspect the movement. Monitors below firing slow at random up the harbor. Majority of garrison reported as having left.

SUMTER, September 7, 1:35 A. M.

September 7, 1:35 A. M.—The assault has been made on Battery Gregg, and I think has been repulsed.

1:55 A. M.—The attack has apparently been repulsed, as our light guns are still firing from Gregg.

2 A. M.—All quiet at Gregg just now, our beach light burning just now.

2:40 A. M.—All the garrison of Morris Island who came here have been shipped. Lieutenant Haskell's boat from the "Chicora," captured by Yankee barge. Two of the crew came to Fort Sumter; report that all our troops had left the island.

Four monitors are engaging the batteries on Sullivan's Island, and firing an occasional shot at Sumter.

The iron-clads still lying off the fort; it is very probable that they will try to remove obstructions with small boats. It would be best if we could throw some light on the obstructions from Sullivan's Island. They fire an occasional shot at the fort wharf.

7:50.—Fleet same as yesterday. Land batteries firing occasionally on Battery Wagner and on Gregg.

SUMTER, September 7, 1863.

A flag of truce from Commodore Dahlgren, demanding the surrender of this fort, has been met by Lieutenant Bowen, of the "Palmetto State." I presume I shall refuse.

SUMTER, September 7.

Extract from Journal kept at post :

Up to this time no direct shots have been fired upon the fort to-day; heavy firing was kept up continually during the day and until 2 A. M. this morning; two monitors had moved up under cover of darkness, and about the time the Morris Island movement began, commenced throwing random shots up the harbor approaches, which they continued during the night. The Morris Island movement was accomplished successfully so far as this post was concerned.* At 8 o'clock A. M. this morning the "Ironsides" and five monitors were near this post, one of the latter quite near; there being a fog seaward, the number of vessels inside the bar and at the other points cannot be accurately counted, but there is no perceptible change since yesterday.

Two monitors have been employed this morning in sounding along Morris Island; they have taken convenient positions for firing at short range at this fort.

I received a communication from Commodore Dahlgren through Lieutenant Bowen, C. S. N., demanding the surrender of this fort; an answer has been sent, stating that a definite reply would be returned as soon as I could communicate with the commander of the department.

Some valuable time has thus been gained.

SUMTER, September 8.

Extract from Journal kept at post :

During yesterday the enemy's land batteries were silent. Early in the morning two monitors came up within short range of the fort, the "Ironsides" and the remaining four monitors taking position near the outer buoy. About 8 A. M. yesterday, a flag of truce was sent by the enemy's fleet, which was met by Lieutenant Bowen, C. S. N. A

---

* The evacuation of Morris Island is referred to.—Q. A. G.

reply to the communication received was subsequently sent by flag of truce from this fort.

At 7 P. M. the "Ironsides" and six monitors engaged Fort Moultrie, throwing an occasional shot at this post, which did no damage except tearing away a small portion of the parapet on the west face. During the night the noise of hammering could be distinctly heard from the parapet, indicating that one of the monitors had been injured and was repairing damages. One of the monitors appears to be aground about twelve hundred yards from Sumter.

There are thirty-six vessels inside the bar, including the "Ironsides" and six monitors.

September 8.—The monitor near Cummings Point is evidently aground, her deck is now four feet above water, and will be some two feet higher at low water. Fire should be opened on her, as the third part of her hull is probably exposed.

9:45 A. M.—The monitor has been hit three times on water line, no change apparent in obstructions.

10:35 A. M.—The monitors have been hit repeatedly; those next Moultrie have drawn her fire from the one aground, which is to be regretted. The "Ironsides" is fourteen hundred and sixty yards from this fort.

11:15 A. M.—"Ironsides" was heavily hit just now, throwing a great deal of sand off her deck. Enemy are busy at their old works on Morris Island. One Parrott gun from there, opened on fort just now.

12 M.—Fragments of "Ironsides" torn away by shot from Sullivan's Island just now.

1:05 P. M.—The "Ironsides" is withdrawing, and one of the monitors has her smoke-stack badly hurt.

SUMTER, September 9.

Extract from Journal kept at post:

About eight (8) o'clock yesterday morning the "Ironsides" and five monitors took positions close to Sullivan's Island and engaged Fort Moultrie and the batteries on that island; they kept up a very severe fire for several hours, our batteries replying promptly. Yesterday morning a monitor was evidently aground near Morris Island; on reporting the fact, Fort Moultrie opened on her, hitting her effectively at least twice; her deck was six feet above the water line, leaving her sides exposed. Shell Point battery also fired on her. It is to be regretted that our fire was not more general and continuous; at high water in the afternoon she got off.

In the engagement of the fleet with Fort Moultrie the monitors were frequently struck, and the "Ironsides" had her deck hit twice, one of the shots tearing away a large portion of her upper bulwarks; she lay alongside of a transport all the afternoon, evidently undergoing repairs.

Having for several nights expected a boat attack, I had one-third of the garrison under arms on the parapet, and the remainder so posted as to reinforce with promptness.

At 1 A. M. this morning, I saw a fleet of barges approaching from the eastward. I ordered the fire to be reserved until they should arrive within a few yards of the fort. The enemy attempted to land on the southeastern and southern faces; he was received by a well-directed fire of musketry, and by hand-grenades, which were very effective in demoralizing him; fragments of the epaulment were also thrown down upon him. The crews near the shore sought refuge in the recesses of the foot of scarp, those further off in flight. The repulse was decided and the assault was not renewed. His force is reported to have been four hundred men, but it is believed to have been much larger. His loss is four men killed, two officers and seventeen men wounded, and ten officers and ninety-two men captured. We secured five stand of colors and five barges; others were disabled and drifted off. One gunboat and Fort Johnson and the Sullivan's Island batteries enfiladed our faces, and contributed to prevent the renewal of the assault. Many of the shots struck the fort. The garrison, consisting of the Charleston Battalion, behaved admirably; all praise is due to Major Blake, his officers and men, for the promptness and gallantry displayed in the defence.

September 9, 4:45 A. M.—Enemy attacked me in barges. We have captured thirteen officers, one hundred and two (102) men, four boats, and three colors. Not one of my men hurt.

One of our gunboats assisted during the fight, unable to communicate with it afterwards.

4:20—Additional two officers captured are First Lieutenant Charles H. Bradford, U. S. Marines, wounded; E. G. Dayton, Executive Officer Wissahickon.

8 A. M.—Enemy sending a flag of truce. I have sent a flag of truce to meet it, stating no flag of truce can be received till explanation is given why they fired upon our flag of truce the other day.

FORT SUMTER, September 10, 1863.

Extract from Journal kept at post :

Everything was very quiet yesterday and last night.

A flag of truce from the enemy's fleet was received at about 9 o'clock A. M. in reference to the prisoners.

Another flag was received at 4 o'clock P. M., bringing baggage belonging to the captured officers and conveniences for the wounded.

A flag was sent from this post to the fleet at about 6 o'clock, bearing despatches from General Jordan, and the bodies of their dead. The prisoners, except the wounded, were sent to the city last night. The "Ironsides," four monitors, and twenty-two other vessels inside the bar.

FORT SUMTER, September 11, 1863.

Extract from Journal kept at post :

Report for 10*th September*, 1863.

Nothing of importance took place yesterday or last night.

Number of vessels inside bar is exactly the same, and they have not changed their positions during the last twenty-four hours.

This morning I notice that the enemy worked industriously at Battery Gregg, and made several additions to that work.

The wounded prisoners were shipped yesterday in a small boat.

A quantity of shot and shell is lying on the wharf ready for shipment, and waiting for transportation.

FORT SUMTER, September 12, 1863.

Extract from Journal kept at post :

Report for 11*th September*, 1863.

Everything has been unusually quiet since yesterday morning. The enemy continues to work at Battery Gregg, and has apparently succeeded in mounting two guns at that point. The batteries on Sullivan's and James Islands kept up a slow fire on Morris Island. The "Ironsides" and six monitors are inside the bar this morning; the number of other vessels is the same as yesterday.

Pursuant to the orders of Brigadier-General commanding, such arms as could be found were sent to the ordnance officer.

FORT SUMTER, September 13, 1863.

Extract from Journal kept at post :

Report of 12*th September*, 1863.

There was no firing yesterday except from our batteries, who gave Morris Island an occasional shot. The enemy is still working at Gregg.

The number of vessels inside the bar has diminished; there are now only two monitors in sight, and the "Ironsides" has dropped lower down. An explosion took place on Morris Island last night, supposed to have been at Battery Wagner.

11:12 A. M.—Please let some adroit person examine the prisoners as to the damage done in Stono by the torpedoes a month ago.

FORT SUMTER, September 14, 1863.

Extract from Journal kept at post:

Report for 13th September, 1863.

The enemy continues to appear inactive except at Battery Wagner, where they are working industriously, altering the fort and mounting guns.

There was no firing at all during the day, except a few shots thrown from our batteries at Morris Island.

There are now inside the bar the "Ironsides," three monitors, and twenty-four other vessels, all lying off the southern portion of Morris Island. The other monitors may not have gone off, but may be concealed behind the hulk of the other vessels.

10:25 A. M.—No working is going on at Battery Gregg. Battery Wagner is being remodelled by a very large party, which is very much exposed. Guns are being mounted there. Continuous shelling should be kept up.

10:30 A. M.—Five monitors in sight, three of which are below.

FORT SUMTER, September 15, 1863.

Extract from Journal kept at post:

Report for 14th September, 1863.

The enemy still appears to be working industriously on Morris Island, chiefly at Wagner, but also at Gregg. Our batteries kept up a very slow fire all day and night. There are now inside the bar the "Ironsides," five monitors, and twenty-six other vessels.

FORT SUMTER, September 16, 1863.

Extract from Journal kept at post:

Report for 15th September, 1863.

There are now inside the bar the "Ironsides," five monitors, two mortar boats, and twenty-five other vessels, two river steamers coming up, and ten blockaders off the bar; also thirty-five in Lighthouse Inlet.

The enemy are still working at Gregg, and exposing themselves with perfect impunity. There was no firing yesterday, except by our batteries and a few shots from Morris Island.

FORT SUMTER, September 17, 1853.

Extract from Journal kept at post:

Report for 16th September, 1863.

Yesterday one banded 42-pounder was thrown on the berm.

There is no material change in the appearance of things on Morris Island. There are now inside the bar the "Ironsides," five monitors, and twenty-five other vessels; they appear to have stood the blow without injury.

12:30 P. M.—Enemy working within four hundred yards southeast of Fort Gregg, perfectly unmolested.

FORT SUMTER, September 18, 1863.

Extract from Journal kept at post:

Report of September 17, 1863.

Apparently no change has taken place in the fleet since my last report.

Yesterday long trains of wagons came down the beach to Gregg, and after discharging their contents, returned again to the upper end of the island. The enemy last night displayed a large calcium light at Cummings Point, its rays were directed on this fort and its approaches. No shot was fired by the enemy yesterday, and only a few were thrown from our batteries at Sullivan's and James Islands.

FORT SUMTER, September 19, 1863.

Extract from Journal kept at post:

Report for September 18, 1863.

The "Ironsides," five monitors, and twenty-five other vessels, are now inside the bar.

The enemy continues to work industriously at Morris Island. A French steamer is off the bar. I shipped a large quantity of shot and some shell in the steamer last night which carried up the two guns; also some iron stripped from gun carriages.

FORT SUMTER, September 20, 1863.

Extract from Journal kept at post:

Report of September 19, 1863.

There are visible this morning within the bar, the "Ironsides," four monitors, and thirty other vessels, mostly schooners; blockaders five. In Lighthouse Inlet twenty-seven vessels.

The change of the garrison was accomplished last night at 10 o'clock P. M.

Mr. Mathews had previously taken off a 7-inch rifle banded.

SUMTER, September 21, 1863.

Extract from Journal kept at post:

Report for September 20, 1863.

The "Ironsides," four monitors, and twenty-nine other vessels within the bar, five propellers outside, and twenty-seven craft in Lighthouse Inlet.

The 10-inch Columbiad at Gregg has been dismounted and rolled over upon the parapet, where it now lies. A monitor was towed out to sea and to the southward yesterday. Wagner is being enlarged and strengthened, heavy parapets are being thrown up facing the northward and westward.

All of the sand hills between Wagner and Gregg are filled with working parties.

[*By Telegraph*, 4:30 P. M.]

The monitor was afterwards towed to the southward, in which direction she disappeared.

I brought from Fort Sumter last night one 42-pounder rifle gun.

(Signed,) J. FRASER MATHEWES.

FORT SUMTER, September 22, 1863.

Extract from Journal kept at post:

Report for 21st September, 1863.

The "Ironsides," four monitors, and thirty other vessels within the bar this morning; thirty in Lighthouse Inlet. Outside, an Englishman, a Frenchman, and seven blockaders, one of which is a frigate. One banded 7-inch was taken to the city last night, and a large quantity of 32-pounder canister and 8-inch shot.

An 8-inch shell gun was placed upon the berm this morning, ready for shipping.

FORT SUMTER, September 23, 1863.

Extract from Journal kept at post:

Report for 22d September, 1863.

The "Ironsides," four monitors, and thirty other vessels within the bar. Two foreigners and five blockaders outside. Usual number in Lighthouse Inlet. Enemy working in large numbers on Wagner, Sandhills, and Gregg. Moultrie is shelling the latter positions, but with little effect. Sand is being carted to the flat beach near Gregg, for the purpose of making a covered way. Our fire has a better effect when directed at Wagner, than at any other point; the working party there is larger, and a discharge from our batteries invariably causes them to seek cover.

[*By Telegraph.*]

I brought from Fort Sumter last night one 32-pounder rifle-banded gun, and placed the same on Commercial wharf.

(Signed,)   J. FRASER MATHEWES.

SUMTER, September 24, 1863.

Extract from Journal kept at post :

Report of 23d September, 1863.

" Ironsides," four monitors, and thirty other vessels inside the bar, seven outside, and about thirty in Lighthouse Inlet. One of the latter shelled the batteries on James Island yesterday for an hour. The enemy still busy on Morris Island, especially at Battery Wagner. Six of the sub-terra torpedoes exploded during the rising of the tide after midnight; the beating of the surf rolled fragments upon them causing their ignition.

[*By Telegraph*, 10 A. M.]

Enemy very hard at work at Wagner, Sandhills, and Gregg. Teams hauling sand for covered way between Gregg and Sandhills. Moultrie firing on new work in latter with small visible effect. Our fire disturbs him more when directed on Wagner than on any other point.

To Colonel HARRIS:

There are here two (2) 10-inch and two (2) 8-inch Columbiads, and only one (1) 8-inch carriage, without elevating screw; two (2) 42-pounder rifled guns, one with band twisted, the other reported in good condition, though still buried in the ruins ; only one (1) 42-pounder carriage, and that with elevating screw gone; one 8-inch shell gun with carriage ; two (2) rifled 32-pounders with carriages, one without; two (2) smooth-bore 32-pounders and one carriage.

(Signed,)   J. A CHAMPNEYS,
Engineer.

I brought away from Fort Sumter last night one 32-pounder banded rifled gun. The northeast wind which has prevailed for the past three or four days has made so rough a sea, that I have been unable to place on the flat, a 10-inch Columbiad and an 8-inch shell gun, which are upon the south and east berm of the fort ready for removal.

(Signed,) J. FRASER MATHEWES.

FORT SUMTER, September 25, 1863.

Extract from Journal kept at post :

Report for 24th September, 1863.

There is no change in the disposition of the fleet this morning, except that one of the monitors lies nearer our works than usual. During the night the enemy have erected a row of palisades around Gregg, and have mounted a large Parrott gun in the new work near Gregg.

[*By Telegraph,* 10 A. M.]

Row of palisades built around Gregg last night; also across the re-entering angle of Wagner. Large Parrott mounted in sand hills near Gregg. What appears to be masked battery nearly completed at Gregg.

[*By Telegraph.*]

I brought from Fort Sumter last night one 10-inch Columbiad.

(Signed,) J. FRASER MATHEWES.

FORT SUMTER, September 26, 1863.

Extract from Journal kept at post :

Report of September 25, 1863.

There are this morning four monitors, the "Ironsides," two mortar boats, and twenty-eight other vessels within the bar; eight outside thirty in Lighthouse Inlet.

Wagner has been extended somewhat to the southward and westward, and Gregg to the southward and eastward. A greal deal was accomplished at both points last night; large detachments of men could be seen moving to and from Gregg, on the beach. At the moment of writing, a shell from Moultrie has killed a horse working at Gregg, and most probably some men.

[*By Telegraph.*]

I brought one 8-inch navy shell gun from Fort Sumter last night. I also got outside one 10-inch mortar, but was compelled to leave it on the wharf by the approach of daylight.

(Signed,)   J. FRASER MATHEWES.

FORT SUMTER, September 27, 1863.

Extract from Journal kept at post:

Report for 26th September, 1863.

There are this morning four monitors, the "Ironsides," two mortar boats, and twenty-seven other vessels within the bar; eight outside, and the usual number in Lighthouse Inlet. A large side-wheel transport has just arrived from southward.

The work on Wagner and Gregg goes vigorously on.

[*By Telegraph.*]

I brought from Fort Sumter last night two 10-inch mortars. I shall proceed to the eastward of Sullivan's Island to-day, to continue the laying of boom obstructions across the mouths of the creeks.

(Signed,)   J. FRASER MATHEWES.

FORT SUMTER, September 28, 1863.

Extract from Journal kept at post:

Report for September 27, 1863.

There are inside the bar this morning same number of vessels as last report; same also outside. The enemy continue to work on Wagner and Gregg, and are still hauling timber for stockades, it is supposed.

Moultrie, Bee, Simkins, and Haskell have been firing at various times in the past twenty-four hours, and have thrown in all one hundred and twenty-six shots; the enemy did not reply.

Battery Simkins fired forty-seven rounds to-day with good effect, it is thought; Battery Cheves was silent, as the magazine at that post is still unfinished.

FORT SUMTER, September 29, 1863.

Extract from Journal kept at post:

Report for September 28, 1863.

At a quarter before two yesterday, land batteries distant two and a third miles opened a slow fire upon this work, directed mainly upon the southwest angle. One hundred shots were thrown, of which forty-eight struck, sixteen fell short, and thirty-six passed over. A negro was killed. The damage to the work is not considerable. A monitor came up apparently to observe the effect of the practice.

This morning the fleet retains the position and numbers of yesterday. The usual amount of work appeared to have been done on Morris Island. The embrasures of Gregg begin to assume the appearance of an evident development towards the city.

[*By Telegraph.*]

Exchange of companies effected last night; covered way thrown from Gregg to sand hills. Southern slope of one of Wagner's faces directed on this point finished and merlons constructed. No water boat came last night. Commander of water boat is an arrant coward, and if the boat is not seized and placed under military control we will not get our full supply of water.

FORT SUMTER, September 30, 1863.

Extract from Journal kept at post:

Report for September 29, 1863.

The fleet diminished by three wooden vessels; one monitor lay near in last night. A quantity of lumber for palisades lies on the beach near Gregg. Four guns have apparently been mounted at Wagner.

The 10-inch Columbiad on the north angle was removed to the parade last night by Mr. Butterfield, and a 42-pounder rifle placed on skids ready for removal to the casemates. During the bombardment yesterday the enemy fired ninety-five shots, of which thirty-four struck without injuring the work materially.

Ninety-four shots fired to-day, of which thirty-five struck. No damage of consequence.

FORT SUMTER, October 1, 1863.

Extract from Journal kept at post:

Report for 30th September, 1863.

The enemy's fire was resumed yesterday at 11:30 A. M.; of sixty-eight shots, forty-five struck, the remainder passed over. Some damage was done to the stairway in the southwest angle. One man was wounded in the face by a fragment of brick.

In the afternoon a long line of men could be observed at Wagner, apparently moving a heavy gun. Two monitors lay in close last night.

* Yesterday morning I placed a 42-rifle, banded, in one of the casemates on the northeast face. Last night Mr. Butterfield threw over on the eastern berm a 42-pounder, and a 10-inch Columbiad with broken trunnion.

A portion of the garrison were employed in constructing cushions to receive them. No marked change has taken place on Morris Island, but there is gradual progress visible.

The enemy's fire war was returned this morning at 8 A. M.

Private J. J. Cranin, Company "I," 11th Regiment South Carolina Infantry, was wounded (slightly) by a fragment of brick.

[*By Telegraph.*]

October 1, 8:15 P. M.—Total number of shots fired by the enemy to-day, sixty-eight (68), forty-five struck, thirty-one (31) inside, and twenty-three (23) passed over. One man slightly wounded on the chin.

FORT SUMTER, October 2, 1863.

Extract from Journal kept at post:

Report for 1st October, 1863.

The "Ironsides," four monitors, two mortar boats, and twenty-five other vessels within the bar; elsewhere the status remains the same.

---

* The following letter contains some information not given circumstantially in the "Journal," and is inserted without comment.—Q. A. G.

CHARLESTON, S. C., *June* 14, 1865.

Maj.-Genl. Q. A. GILLMORE, *Comdg. Dept. South:*

GENERAL :—In reply to your queries, proposed for the purpose of affording aid to military history and science, I have the honor to state:

1*st*. That when I assumed command of Fort Sumter on the 4th of September, 1863, there were no guns in position except one 32-pounder in one of the northwest casemates. This gun was merely used for firing at sunset, and was not intended for any other purpose.

In the early portion of October I mounted in the northeast casemates two 10-inch Columbiads and one 7-inch rifle. In January one 8-inch and two 7-inch rifles were mounted in the northwest casemates; one of them was, I have understood, removed after I was relieved from command of the fort.

2*d*. I had no official connection with the channel obstructions. The floating network appeared most perfect early in September. Soon afterwards several sections floated away or sunk. I never regarded the torpedoes said to be placed in the channel-way as of much value. I have always regarded Charleston to have been most exposed to a naval attack during the month of September, 1863.

I am, very respectfully,
Your obedient,
STEPHEN ELLIOTT,
Brig.-Genl. late C. S. A.,
And formerly commanding Fort Sumter.

Appearances on Morris Island suggest permanent occupation rather than immediate operations; all the high sand hills on the southern end of the Island are strongly entrenched. Wagner is being extended still more to the southwest; two siege and two barbette guns are mounted upon one of her faces looking towards this fort.

The firing commenced earlier yesterday; out of one hundred and twenty-nine (129) shots, seventy-five (75) struck. The monitors perform picket-duty nightly.

All the enemy's movements by land and water show caution and fear of surprise.

FORT SUMTER, October 3, 1863.

Extract from Journal kept at post :

Report for 2d October, 1863.

The "Ironsides," four monitors, two mortar boats, and twenty-five other vessels inside the bar; elsewhere the status remains the same.

The firing commenced at 8 o'clock A. M. yesterday morning; out of seventy-four shots, forty-four struck, two of which penetrated the gorge wall near the old officers' quarters; no other material damage done to the work.

At 8 o'clock A. M. this morning, the enemy's batteries were opened again.

FORT SUMTER, October 4, 1863.

Extract from Journal kept at post:

Report for 3d October, 1863.

The usual number of vessels below this morning. Out of ninety-five shots yesterday, seventy-eight struck the fort. The injury was immaterial, except that the top of the breach was knocked off. Captain Lloyd's Company, "B," 25th South Carolina Volunteers, thirty-one men, relieved Captain Kaysor's Company, "H," 11th South Carolina Volunteers, sixty-three men, last night.

The enemy are still at work on the northeast face of Wagner.

] FORT SUMTER, October 5, 1863.

Extract from Journal kept at post :

Report of October 4, 1863.

There is no material change in the fleet off the harbor this morning. Three hundred and seventeen shots have been fired by our batteries

---

* This refers to October 1, but differs by six (6) shot from the number reported by telegraph.—Q. A. G.

(Sullivan's Island, Simkins, Cheves, and Haskell) since 6 A. M. yesterday. The enemy have fired in the same time one hundred and thirty-six shots.

Several large vessels arrived to-day from the northward, laden, but it is not believed they brought any troops, probably loaded with ordnance stores.

A small submarine affair was observed to-day with the fleet, and was towed over the bar, and brought inside by one of the blockading vessels.

Monitor No. 5 is off the bar.

FORT SUMTER, October 6, 1863.

No visible change in fleet this morning.

The enemy have made and are still making great improvements in Wagner and Gregg.

Captain Gaillard's company reported last night, numbering fifty (50) men.

[*By Telegraph.*]

I have four floating torpedoes in Charleston ready for use. Can you order Sergeant S. E. Barnwell and four men of the Beaufort Artillery from Pocotaligo, to operate with them.

There are two (2) submarine affairs near the "Ironsides;" there are also several wooden gunboats close in. Look out for some tricks to-night.

The "Ironsides" has not been injured apparently.

FORT SUMTER, October 7, 1863.

No change in fleet. The monitor seen off the bar on the 5th inst., has taken position inside, and one of those here previously is not to be seen. They are probably going to Port Royal in turn, to be overhauled.

Work is going on as usual on Morris Island. Can you send down a casemate gin or some jackscrews, for the purpose of mounting the guns?

FORT SUMTER, October 8, 1863.

No change in fleet. Two shots were fired last night by the monitor on advanced post, at a schooner containing sand bags, lying between Sumter and Battery Bee; musketry from the fleet was also heard.

A large Parrott has been mounted in Gregg, in the embrasure directed upon this fort; the breach of the gun, however, lies this way. The half-moon battery in the sand hills I take to be a mortar battery.

A 42-rifle, banded, was mounted here yesterday, and a 10-inch placed in position, ready for mounting. Some necessary alterations in the chassis delayed the operation last night.

FORT SUMTER, October 9, 1863.

But little change this morning, with the exception of a gradual advance in the completion of the batteries on Morris Island.

A wide embrasure at Gregg, directed towards this place, is being revetted, as is also the half-moon battery on the sand hills.

Our fire was effective yesterday; casualties were seen to take place both at Gregg and Wagner.

FORT SUMTER, October 10, 1863.

No change in fleet. Work is going on as usual at Morris Island. Musketry was heard last night from the fleet.

The Parrott gun mounted at Gregg remains still with the breech towards this work.

FORT SUMTER, October 10, 1863.

CAPTAIN:

I have the honor to send you two (2) prisoners, John M. Smith and John Wonser, who were captured by our post-boat to-night, on its way from Fort Johnson to this place. I have secured their boat, which is of convenient size for use at this post, and their arms. No very important facts have been elicited by their examination.

FORT SUMTER, October 11, 1863.

No material change in fleet or shore this morning.

A detachment of five men, under command of Sergeant S. E. Barnwell, of the Beaufort Artillery, sent down four floating torpedoes last night; a heavy explosion took place at the proper time in the fleet, but no result was apparent this morning.

At 8 o'clock last night the post-boat coming from Fort Johnson overhauled a small boat containing two of the enemy, who surrendered immediately. They were evidently expecting a friendly boat, whether from the city or not is uncertain.

Is it well that this portion of the harbor should be without an armed patrol of some sort? The prisoners were sent up under a guard last night.

A 10-inch was placed upon the wharf last night.

FORT SUMTER, October 12, 1863.

Inside bar "Ironsides," four monitors, and twenty-four other vessels; outside seven, and nineteen in Lighthouse Inlet.

The slopes on Battery Wagner have a finished appearance, but are not revetted as yet; a salient directed to the westward is being pushed forwards at Gregg, and the curtain between that fort and the half-moon battery is being strengthened. Carriage and chassis for second 10-inch arrived, and will be moved into position as rapidly as possible.

FORT SUMTER, October 13, 1863.

One schooner added to fleet this morning. Five blockaders in sight.

Affairs on Morris Island appear unchanged. There has been less visible activity there yesterday than on any previous occasion.

FORT SUMTER, October 14, 1863.

Condition of fleet unchanged. The command of the western salient at Gregg is being much increased. A new battery has been commenced to the eastward of, and near to the half-moon battery.

The second 10-inch Columbiad was mounted last night in our casemate battery.

The "Ironsides" is in her usual position. One monitor is near here, two others lower down; the fourth not visible.

FORT SUMTER, October 16, 1863.

"Ironsides," four monitors, three mortar boats, and twenty-three other craft within the bar; five blockaders outside, and nineteen vessels in Stono.

Judging by the ventilators, an extensive bomb-proof has been built at Gregg. A number of carts may be seen passing behind the covered way. The battery reported yesterday is progressing, and a heavy force is at work on what was the old bomb-proof at Wagner.

The detachment of thirty men from Captain Harleston's company was returned last night by steamer "Etiwan," as also some of the iron collected by them at the fort. The presence of a schooner with sand prevented as large a shipment of iron as was advisable.

FORT SUMTER, October 16, 1813.

"Ironsides," four monitors, and twenty-two other vessels inside the bar; seven blockaders outside, and nineteen craft in Lighthouse Inlet.

No marked change has taken place on Morris Island since yesterday.

FORT SUMTER, October 17, 1863.

No change in fleet, except that the fourth monitor cannot be seen, being probably masked by one of the other vessels. The improvement of earthworks on Morris Island is steady. A lot of iron and coal was shipped for the city and Sullivan's Island last night.

FORT SUMTER, October 18, 1863.

Condition of fleet unchanged this morning; the fourth monitor has not been discovered, though she may be concealed by some of the other vessels.

The progress of the enemy on the battery next the half-moon battery is very rapid; the disposition of their batteries indicate at present operations against Sullivan's Island.

Companies "I" and "K," Eleventh South Carolina Regiment, were relieved last night by the Twelfth Georgia battery, Major Harvey, two hundred and eighteen men. A lot of coal was shipped by the Etiwan last night, the remainder will be sent on Monday night.

FORT SUMTER, October 19, 1863.

Five monitors in sight, one of them outside; in other respects the fleet remains about the same. The batteries on Morris Island are advancing, though no new developments have been made since yesterday's report. A few shots from heavy guns were heard at sea last night. At dawn this morning all the wooden gunboats now lying inside, were observed to enter the bar and resume their usual anchorage.

FORT SUMTER, October 20, 1863.

"Ironsides," five monitors, and twenty-four other vessels inside this morning; six outside, one of them a large wooden gunboat that arrived from the southward, and twenty-two in Lighthouse Inlet.

Land operations continue as usual. Entrenchments have been commenced in the rear of the half-moon battery; their exact nature cannot as yet be ascertained. Large shipments of sand were received last night. The wharf was so crowded thereby that no coal or iron could be sent off.

FORT SUMTER, October 21, 1863.

The new batteries on Morris Island continue to increase in dimension. No correct report can be made of the fleet this morning on account of the fog. Two of the enemy's picket boats were observed last night between this post and Gregg; information was extended to Major Blanding, who fired upon them with grape, but the range was too great.

A flat-boat loaded with coal, shot, and iron, was sent up last night.

FORT SUMTER, October 22, 1863.

Four monitors in the harbor this morning. One of them has a network of wire surrounding, and probably covering the forward half of the deck.

The "Ironsides" has three stout beams projecting obliquely from her bow downwards into the water. They are probably braces to some torpedo or anti-torpedo device. One of the mortar boats has been towed outside, and now lies near the "Wabash." In other respects the fleet is as usual.

The land batteries are being pushed forwards vigorously. Their working parties suffer (?) greatly from the want of being shelled. The flat was not sent back last night, and a large amount of iron is lying on the wharf ready for shipment.

FORT SUMTER, October 23, 1863.

The thick weather prevents any accurate observations this morning. A second heavy gun is, however, visible at Gregg, and appears to bear upon this position.

FORT SUMTER, October 24, 1863.

Inside bar, "Ironsides," four monitors, one mortar boat, and twenty other vessels; five blockaders and twenty-four craft in Lighthouse Inlet. No new earthworks are being thrown up, but those already in hand are being rapidly pushed forward.

The steamer "Randolph" with a raft of logs in tow, allowed herself to be taken by the tide past the fort last night. After some time, being discovered and fired upon by a monitor, she was compelled to cut the logs adrift and return to the wharf.

About fifty discharges of small arms from the beach near the Moultrie House were observed at 9 P. M. last night.

DEFENCE OF FORT SUMTER.

FORT SUMTER, October 25, 1863.

State of fleet is to-day the same in every respect as yesterday, except that the number of the blockaders is reduced to three, and there are three tugs outside near the "Wabash."

At Gregg portions of three guns can be seen. One bears upon this point, a second upon this point and Fort Johnson, and the third upon Fort Johnson. At sunset yesterday there was heavy firing from a blockader, some ten miles to the northward and eastward.

While the "Ironsides" was lying in a certain position yesterday, it was apparent that the structure under her bow extended also some distance on her side. This renders it probable that it is a defensive arrangement.

Six hundred and seventy-nine (679) shots fired, eighty-eight missed. Made a breach in sea-face, knocking down the arches; cut the gorge wall very thin on top.

FORT SUMTER, October 26, 1863.

"Ironsides," four monitors, and a mortar boat, and twenty-four other vessels inside. Two blockaders outside, and eighteen vessels of all sorts in Lighthouse Inlet. No material change has been observed on Morris Island, except that the large Parrott gun at Gregg has at last been turned with the muzzle towards this point.

One hundred and eighty-eight shots from Morris Island. One hundred and sixty-five (165) struck, twenty-three (23) passed over. Ten shots fired from monitors.

4:30.—Enemy have opened upon us from Gregg, Wagner, and centre battery. We are all right.

FORT SUMTER, October 27, 1863.

Number of vessels inside has been reduced by three, while two have been added to the list in Lighthouse Inlet. At half-past twelve yesterday Battery Gregg, the middle battery, and Wagner opened upon us, firing one hundred and eighty-eight (188) shots, of which one hundred and sixty-five (165) struck, making some impression upon the gorge wall, upon which their fire is directed. In the afternoon a wooden gunboat steamed up to the two monitors lying at their usual picket station. One of the latter and the gunboat fired nine shots, one of which penetrated the sand bag traverse above the hospital, and wounded a negro. No other casualties occurred from the fire. There are two guns at Gregg bearing upon us, and embrasures in the curtain for two more. There is a 300-pounder in the middle battery and two smaller guns. I cannot distinctly ascertain the number at Wagner, although there appears to be about five in position for us. Most of their guns being in embrasure, it is evident from their direction that their intention is to operate regularly against this work.

The powder has been removed from the old magazine, and a part placed in the new magazine near the casemate battery; the remainder in the bomb-proof near the old sally-port. Major Pringle took off the flat with iron last night. It is not advisable to send it back at present.

October 27.

The enemy's fire was very damaging to the sea-face, breaching the traverses in the upper arches. The gorge wall is also cut to a thin edge in some places. The land batteries and fleet fired six hundred and twenty-five shots. Lieutenant Brown, Georgia Battalion, dangerously hurt. No other serious casualties.

FORT SUMTER, October 28, 1863.

Six hundred and seventy-nine shots fired against the fort last night, eighty-eight of which missed. A breach was made in the sea-face, knocking down the arches, and the top of the gorge wall was cut very thin.

FORT SUMTER, October 29, 1863.

Not a captain of the Georgia Battalion is present. Captain Ruddesell, Co. "B," went off to Fort Johnson night before last, on certificate of his brother the surgeon, without my knowledge. Captain Anderson is on court-martial on James Island. Captain Hood, Co. "F," Captain G. H. Hodd, and Captain F. N. Taliaferro, Co. "D," are both at Augusta on sick leave. I have good reason to believe that neither of those three who are reported sick are unfit for duty. Unless I have my company commanders I cannot be responsible for the result of a night attack. Please send this at once to the Commanding General.

FORT SUMTER, October 29, 1863.

Enemy fired seven hundred and seventy-nine (779) shots, eighty missed. The top row of arches on sea-face cut down. The whole of that face and the gorge perfectly accessible from the outside. One man killed on post.

DEFENCE OF FORT SUMTER. 127

FORT SUMTER, October 30, 1863.

Haze prevents accurate report of fleet. Seven hundred and seventy-nine shots fired at fort yesterday. Eighty passed over. Effect, etc. (*vide* telegram of preceding day). Two hundred and sixty shots fired last night. Eighty missed. This makes one thousand and thirty-nine (1,039) of all calibres, from 15-inch monitor and 300-pounder Parrotts downwards. From present direction of enemy's fire, I am led to conclude that he wishes to avoid injuring the northeast and city faces of the work as much as possible. Think he will try an assault.

Fort Moultrie can sweep our sea-face, but there is no enfilade fire for the gorge wall. Unless a gunboat can be placed in position beforehand between this post and Fort Johnson, their assistance will be useless, as the success of an assault will be determined in a very few minutes. It would be all important to have a guard-boat stationed between this fort and Cummings Point, which could signal the approach of barges; another stationed to seaward for same purpose would be of a great advantage. I recognize the perilous nature of this service, but is not the holding of this post worth some little risk?

Private H. C. Castlebury, Co. "B," 12th Ga. Battalion, was killed while on post yesterday, by the explosion of a 15-inch shell. Private B. Griffin, Co. "A," 12th Ga., slightly wounded in hand. Private Z. Stanford, same company, slightly wounded in leg. Private A. Williams, Co. "A," stunned. Private Beardin, same company, wounded in shoulder. Private T. Goggins, Co. "K," 1st S. C. Art'y; slightly in head. Sergeant A. Freeman, Co. "A," 12th Ga. Battalion, slightly. Flagstaff shot away after retreat.

I was enabled to keep strong guard on the parapet last night, and the main body within a few yards in readiness to move immediately.

The cutting of the Keokuk angle still continues; the greater portion of the fire this morning is done by mortars. Three men slightly wounded this morning.

Please apply to Commanding General to order by telegraph Lieutenant E. J. Tutt, Co. "F," Twelfth Georgia Battalion, to rejoin his command here; he is at Augusta, Georgia.

6:30.—Number of shot fired at Sumter from sun-up to sun-down on the 30th, to-day, nine hundred and fifty-five (955), sixty-eight (68) of which missed.

7:30.—No casualties since those reported this morning. Still more accessible from outside; interior communication considerably broken up.

FORT SUMTER, October 31, 1863.

10:25.—The firing to-day was from two monitors, and from two heavy and two light rifled guns at Gregg, from three heavy rifled guns and four 10-inch mortars at the middle battery, and from four medium rifled guns at Wagner. Four hundred and forty-three rifled shots were fired, of which sixty-one missed; eighty-six shots fired from monitors, all reported as having struck, and three hundred and seventy-three mortar shells, of which one hundred and twenty missed.

Sergeant W. C. Owens, Sergeant J. A. Stevens, privates S. L. Burrows, F. M. Burrows, S. W. Anderson, Jas. Calder, O. J. Burn, W. E. Gibson, J. W. Jones, L. S. Lee, and W. N. Patterson of W. L. I., Co. "A," Twenty-fifth Regiment, Private W. Martin of Twelfth Georgia battery, and Mr. Matthews an overseer, were buried this morning by the falling in of the barracks on the sea-face, where they had been placed in position for mounting the parapet in case of an assault.

Land batteries and three monitors fired in all, yesterday, nine hundred and fifty-five shot and shell, sixty of which missed; during the night sixty-eight were fired, eight of which missed; making an aggregate of one thousand and twenty shots in the twenty-four hours. At three o'clock this morning a Parrott shell struck an iron girder in the sea-wall, and a moment after the roof fell in, crushing thirteen men who were posted there in readiness for an immediate mount to the crest in case of a boat attack. The position was considered comparatively safe as the roof had resisted the shock of the falling debris. It is a matter of serious regret that my recommendation for the construction of a capacious bomb-proof, soon after assuming command, was not adopted by the Engineer Department. It will be a matter of difficulty to repel the enemy should he advance this way. I would be glad to receive eight or ten ladders fifteen feet in length to-night, to enable me to mount more rapidly.

FORT SUMTER, November 1, 1863.

The fire yesterday proceeded from two monitors, etc. (*vide* telegram of Oct. 31). Two mortar fuses are cut so as to explode the shell a second or two after impact. During the night seventy rifled shots were fired, mostly with time fuses, of which ten passed over, and thirty-three mortar shells, twelve of which did not strike. The fire of the land batteries was directed chiefly at the southwest angle, which suffered severely. The flagstaff was shot away twice, and replaced by Sergeant Graham, Corporal Hitt, and Private R. Swain, all of Co. "F," Twelfth Georgia battery. The flagstaff was so cut up that it was necessary to raise the battle flag of the Twelfth Georgia Battalion in the place of the flag. The following is a list of the casualties: During yesterday, Private Jno. Myers, Co. "F," killed by mortar shell; Private Melton Gibbes, same company, killed at the same time; Private M. W. Wilkes, Co. "D," Twelfth Georgia Battalion, fracture of jaw bone; Private David Hughes, Co. "F," same corps, wounded severely in back; Private A. Honour and Corporal F. H. Honour, Co. "A," Twenty-fifth C. S. V., all by mortar shells.

9:30 A. M.—We are getting on well; no further casualties.

10:40 A. M.—During the night seventy rifled shots were fired at this post, ten of which missed; thirty-three mortars, twelve of which missed. Most of rifled shots were from 30-pounders with time fuses. Fire heavy on southwest angle; our cover at that point, however, still safe. However, traverses above the hospital penetrated in one spot. No casualties to-day.

12:15 P. M.—As another nomination might supersede Barnwell, and as he is the man I want, I would prefer waiting a few days, in which time I hope he will have recovered.

FORT SUMTER, November 2, 1863.

Fire of enemy was directed mainly at the southwest angle yesterday, which he succeeded in breaching on the outside, but not to an extent to make the protection within insecure as yet. Monitors opened upon the sea-wall, and in reverse upon the city face, doing some damage in the region of the new sally-port. Owing to the difficulty of observing the monitors during their period of action, an accurate estimate of the number of shots from them was not obtained: it bore, however, about the same proportion to the number of shots from the land batteries as on the previous day. The number of these shots computed with the land guns was three hundred and seventy-five (375), of which forty-six (46) missed. The number of mortar shells fired was three hundred and eight (308), of which eighty-seven (87) missed. The number last night was fifty-four (54) rifled shell, of which seven (7) missed, and four (4) mortar shell, of which two (2) missed. The number of projectiles of all kinds fired since Monday last is five thousand five hundred and sixty-five (5,565), of which eight hundred and seventeen (817) missed, and four thousand seven hundred and forty-eight (4,748) struck. I beg leave to call your attention to the fact that for the second time the movement to relieve a portion of the garrison failed of accomplishment, and to urge that some remedy be applied. Learning that the troops detailed to relieve the companies of the Twentieth S. C. V., were awaiting transportation at Fort Johnson, I sent over Captain Carson's company in my mail boat after its arrival from Charleston, making two trips, and bringing over one officer and fourteen men of the relief. The non-fulfilment of official promises is to be regretted, as it shows a want of confidence on the part of the troops. The only casualties yesterday happened to W. Hallick, private, Co. "D," Georgia Battalion, who was wounded slightly in the leg.

[*By Telegraph.*]

One hundred and forty (140) shots from the monitors, all struck. Two hundred and fifty (250) rifle shots from Morris Island, fifty-five (55) of which missed. Three hundred and forty-five (345) mortar shells, of which an hundred and thirty-five (135) missed. One man killed by mortar shell.

I consider the damage done to the fort as a defensive position is perhaps less to-day than on any day of the bombardment.

Although the crest of the southwest angle has been much cut, the disjoined masses have assumed a favorable position for the defence of the lower casemates. Besides 15-inch shell the monitors fire rifle shell, nineteen (19) inches long, and six and a half ($6\frac{1}{2}$) inches in diameter, of the pattern styled "Wiard."

Send us some fresh beef.

FORT SUMTER, November 3, 1863.

Bombardment continued as usual yesterday, the monitors relieving the heavy guns on Morris Island. About noon, one hundred and forty (140) 15-inch and $6\frac{1}{4}$-inch rifle shot were fired from the monitors, all of which struck.

Two hundred and fifty (250) rifled shot from Morris Island, fifty-five (55) of which missed, and three hundred and forty-five (345) mortar shells, one hundred and thirty-five (135) of which missed. During the night eighty-seven (87) rifle shots were fired, thirty-six (36) of which missed, and five (5) mortar shell which fell in.

The upper portion of the scarp on the southwest angle is cut away, but the fragments have assumed the natural shape, and contribute to the safety of the lower casemates. Immediately after dark a small boat containing four (4) of the enemy's scouts, made a landing at the southeast angle. The darkness having prevented its approach from being observed, and our sentinels not believing that it could be an enemy, hailed, and allowed the party to escape, although the officer in command states that several shots struck the boat during its retreat. The delay in firing was due to the fact that there was only one boat, and that it was known that a picket boat was assigned to this station.

The Infantry garrison was relieved by a detachment of two officers and forty (40) men from each of the following regiments: 6th, 19th, 23d, 27th, 28th Georgia, and by Companies "C" and "D," 25th South Carolina Volunteers, ninety-six (96) men.

The different portions of the garrison have been assigned permanently to separate posts of the work, which it is hoped will contribute to the certainty of a repulse.

The only casualty yesterday was the death of Private Calvin Giles, Company "B," 12th Georgia Battalion, by the explosion of mortar shell.

[*By Telegraph.*]

8:45 P. M.—The monitors fired one hundred and fourteen (114) shots to-day, none of which are reported to have missed.

Two hundred and seventy-seven (277) rifled shots were fired, forty (40) of which missed, and one hundred and seventy-eight (178) mortar shell, of which seventeen (17) missed. One mortar shell penetrated the casemate battery and exploded, wounding three men, not seriously. The traverses above the hospital were penetrated, and the top of the shell room on the southwest angle breached.

8:45 P. M.—At the suggestion of Colonel Rhett, I recommend that palisades be prepared in the city and sent down to assist in the defence of the slopes of this work.

I respectfully recommend that a promise of a furlough of ten days be held out to my garrison in the event of their repelling a heavy assault upon the work. It would contribute more powerfully to the success of the defence than any measure I can think of.

FORT SUMTER, November 4, 1863.

The fire from the fleet and batteries continued yesterday. Monitors fired one hundred and fourteen (114) shots, all of which are reported to have struck. Morris Island fired two hundred and seventy-seven (277) rifled shot, forty (40) of which missed, and one hundred and seventy eight (178) mortar shell, of which seventeen (17) missed. During the night ninety-two (92) 30-pounder rifled shots with time fuses were fired, all of which except fifteen (15) exploded over and within the fort. The practice with these projectiles is very beautiful; the adjustment of the time being so perfect that the occupants of the gorge wall are secure from the effects of the explosion, which rarely fails to occur during the passage of the shell over the parade. The fire was directed yesterday upon the southwest angle, the upper casemate of which was breached, and in reverse upon the city face, the northern portion of which was somewhat cut, and the traverse over the hospital partly knocked down. On the whole, damage was not great. Captain W. H. Peronneau, Company "G," 1st S. C. Artillery, forty (40) men, relieved Lieutenant Lowndes, Company "K," same corps, forty (40) men.

The following is a list of the casualties yesterday from the explosion of a mortar shell which accidentally found its way into the battery. Privates Wm. B. Eates, Company "E," B. F. Morris, Company "H," J. A. Smith, Company "D," Jas. Chambers and J. R. Morris, Company "E," 27th Georgia.

Concussion from explosion of shell in battery, Private J. R. Stephens, Company "E."

[*By Telegraph.*]

Number of shots fired to-day: Monitors, eighty-six, all hit; rifle shots, two hundred, twenty-six missed; mortars, one hundred and thirty-six, thirty-six missed.

FORT SUMTER, November 5.

On night of 4th, eighty-six rifled shots fired, forty struck. Day of 5th, two hundred shots fired, one hundred and fifty-seven struck; mortars, two hundred and thirteen fired, one hundred and seventy-three struck; monitors, seventy-eight fired, all struck. Night of 5th, fifty-eight rifled shots fired, thirty-seven struck; mortar shell, one struck. Day of 8th, ninety-three rifled shots fired, sixty struck; one hundred and eighty-eight mortar shells fired, one hundred and forty-three struck; eleven shots from monitors, six struck. Night of 8th, fifty-eight rifled shot fired, forty-two struck.

FORT SUMTER, November 6, 1863.

During the night fifty-eight (58) shots, of which twenty-one (21) missed; monitor, one struck. The fire of land batteries was directed on southwest angle, upon which the effect was not very considerable. The fire of the monitors was directed on the eastern pan-coupé. The crown of eastern arch was destroyed; the debris fell in and arrested the work of the engineers. Private A. Lavender, Company "F," 25th Georgia Regiment, severe flesh wound by fragments of shell in the back.

7 P. M.—The flagstaff was shot down to-day and was replaced by Sergeant W. D. Currie, Company "D," and Corporal S. Montgomery, Company "C," 25th S. C. V. The following is the number of casualties: ten men slightly wounded, two severely, and two killed, all of the 27th Georgia.

FORT SUMTER, November 7, 1863.

Bombardment continued yesterday to the following extent: Rifled shots fired from land batteries, one hundred and fifty-three (153), of which thirty-one (31) missed; mortar shells, one hundred and ninety-three (193), of which thirty-four missed: monitors fired eighty (80), of which fourteen (14) missed. During the night sixty-eight (68) light rifle shells were fired from Gregg, twenty-nine (29) of which either failed to explode or exploded after passing over. The fire of the monitors was directed upon the east angle and upon the scarp of the northeast face, to which it did some injury. Is it impracticable to annoy the monitors when in position, from Sullivan's Island? Another monitor shell found its way into the battery yesterday and exploded, wounding several men slightly. Another mortar shell exploded at the eastern entrance of main and bomb-proof, and killed two and wounded several. The following is a list of the killed and wounded:

Privates Howell and Jones, Company "B," 28th Ga., killed; private Robert Vance, Company "B" 28th Ga., killed; private Henry Suttlefield, Company "G," 1st S. C. Art'y, slight; private Aaron Bates, Company "G," 1st S. C. Art'y, hip, severe; private John Burton, Company "G," 1st S C. Art'y, thigh, slight; private W. J. Butler, Company "E," 28th Ga., foot, severe; private S. C. Lawrence, Company "B," 28th Ga., scalp, slight; private J. T. Salter, Company "H," 28th Ga., concussion; private John Norrill, Company "G," 28th Ga., concussion; private Jonis A. Lam, Company "G," 28th Ga., concussion; private James D. Emery, Company "F," 28th Ga., concussion; private Henry Wood, Company "B," 28th Ga., concussion; private Peter Wood, Company "B," 28th Ga., concussion; private H. W. Lawrence, Company "B," 28th Ga., concussion.

Last night Captain Rentfro, with one lieutenant and twenty-four men from the 27th Ga., Lieutenant Mathews, 6th Ga., thirty-four men, Lieutenant Smith, 28th Ga., thirty-three men, relieved detachments of forty and twenty men and three officers from 27th, 6th, and 28th Ga., respectively. The captains of two of these detachments whose time had expired were retained for twenty-four hours for the purpose of assisting the new officers, strangers to the work, in the discharge of their duties. Captain J. Johnson arrived for the purpose of relieving Captain Champneys, engineer.

November 7.

The following is the number of shots fired to-day: Rifle, fired seventy-one (71), missed fifteen (15); mortars, fired two hundred and twelve (212), missed forty-six (46).

FORT SUMTER, November 8, 1863.

During the night sixty-three (63) time shells were fired, of which sixteen (16) missed. The injury done to the work was perhaps less marked than on any previous day.

The following casualties occurred:

First Lieutenant David Waters, Co. "G," 1st S. C. Art'y, concussion, slight.

Private Thomas Watts, Co. "C," 28th Ga., forearm and hand, severe.

Private J. M. Page, Co. "B," 29th Ga., contusion of side, slight.

The Mountain howitzer, though placed in a position of supposed security, was struck in the chase by a fragment of a mortar shell, causing a convexity in the bore. This, I think, can be removed by boring out. The piece was sent out per steamer "Randolph," last night, and contains a round of case shot. I append a condensed statement of the work performed by Engineer Department on the night of November 7th and 8th, as submitted by Capt. Johnson, Engineer in charge: Force (170) one hundred and seventy hands. Discharged twenty-seven hundred (2700) sand bags of sand and some timber. Repaired, raised, and enlarged traverse over west circular stairway; filled mortar holes in gorge, bomb-proof, and traverse in rear of north-east lower casemate battery. Carpenters worked on ladders, ventilators, and chevaux-de-frise, being obliged to remodel the latter. No wire fencing yet built on the expected posts, and frames have not yet arrived from the city.

DEFENCE OF FORT SUMTER.

[*By Telegraph.*]

I have the honor to report the following number of shots fired: Rifle, fired ninety-three (93), of which twenty-three missed (23); mortars, fired one hundred and eighty-eight (188), of which forty-five (45) missed; monitors, fired eleven (11), of which five (5) missed. One negro severely, and one dangerously wounded. No further damage.

FORT SUMTER, November 9, 1863.

During the night fifty-eight (58) rifled shots were fired, of which sixteen (16) missed. The fire of the land batteries during the day was directed chiefly upon the southwest angle, without serious damage; that of the monitors upon the scarp wall of the northeast face, which was not materially injured.

Recapitulation of the week.

Rifled from land batteries fired	1,803
Missed	411
From mortars fired	1,467
Missed	359
From monitors fired	471
Missed	19
Total fired	3,741
Total struck	2,952
Total missed	789
Total fired during previous week five thousand five hundred and sixty-five	5,565
Total struck	4,748
Total missed	817
Aggregate fired since the opening of the present bombardment, nine thousand three hundred and six	9,306
Struck	7,700
Missed	1,606

I have to correct an error into which I was led by the report of an officer detailed to take the measurement of the rifled projectiles fired from the monitors. Their correct diameter is eight (8) inches, and not six and a-half (6½), as was reported; length twenty (20) inches. Five (5) negroes were wounded yesterday by the explosion of a mortar shell, and by bricks thrown by a rifled shell at night, one dangerously, one severely, and three (3) slightly. I add condensed statement of work done, submitted by Captain Johnson, Engineer in charge: Force: one hundred and sixty (160); discharged, seventeen hundred (1,700) filled sand bags, filled mortar-shell holes over ventilators above and in rear of battery; repaired bomb-proof cone over stairway of southwest angle; began combing west end of gorge bomb proof chevaux-de-frise along three-fourths of sea slope; spiked plank along east half of gorge slope; former taken in before day by garrison; no frames yet arrived for iron fence; they shall be made here, if not sent to-night.

On night of the 4th eighty-six rifled shots fired, sixty (60) of which struck. During the day of the 5th, two hundred (200) rifled shots fired, one hundred and fifty-seven (157) of which struck; mortars fired, two hundred and thirteen (213), one hundred and seventy-three (173) of which struck. Monitors fired seventy-eight (78), all of which struck. During night of 5th fifty-eight (58) rifled shots fired, thirty-seven (37) of which struck. Mortars fired one shell, which*struck. During night of 8th ninety-three (93) rifled shots fired, sixty (60) of which struck. One hundred and eighty-eight (188) mortar shells fired, one hundred and forty-three (143) of which struck. Eleven (11) shots fired by monitors, six (6) of which struck. During night of 8th fifty-eight (58) rifled shots fired, forty-two (42) of which struck.

The following is the number of shots fired to-day:

Rifled, sixty-one (61), of which twenty (20) missed. Mortars fired, twenty-five (25), of which five (5) missed. Monitors fired, twenty-five (25), of which seven (7) missed.*

FORT SUMTER, November 10, 1863.

Following number of shots was fired yesterday: Rifle, sixty-one (61), of which twenty-one (21) missed. Monitors, twenty-five (25), of which seven missed * Mortar shelling by night was resorted to for the first time since the commencement of the bombardment. The rifle practice was also more frequent than on previous nights. Number of shots from rifle one hundred and fifty-four, missed sixty-two. From mortars one hundred and eighty-two, missed fifty. The heavy guns from

---

* All the above-mentioned shots are included in the "Recapitulation of the week," under date of November 9.

the land have ceased their fire to a great extent. The rifle practice is conducted almost exclusively from light pieces. Day firing has in like manner given way to night. This may indicate that their heavy ammunition has been much reduced, and their heavy guns endangered. They may have resorted to night firing as a means of covering an assault, which I think will probably be attempted within the present week, as the bright nights will, after that period, have come in. I have the honor again to direct your attention to the propriety of assigning Trenholm's section of howitzers to duty at this post.

The only casualty yesterday was the wounding of Private M. A. Brown, Co. " C," 25th S. C. Vols., slightly, in the foot and ankle.

The post boat broke from its moorings last night, and drifted away. The telegraphic cable was cut by a shell at a distance of about fifty feet from the fort; communication has therefore been suspended.

Captain Johnson, Engineer in charge, reports that no sand bags arrived last night. Force repaired top of traverse in rear of battery; resumed filling ordnance store room, southwest angle; placed chevaux-de-frise along the whole of east slope.

FORT SUMTER, November 11, 1863.

Following number of shots fired yesterday: Rifled, forty-six (46), of which eight (8) missed; mortar shells fifty (50), of which twenty-five (25) missed; monitors, thirty (30), of which nine (9) missed.

No casualties occurred. A detachment of one hundred men and ten officers, under the command of Captain Crawford, of the 17th S. C. V., relieved a detachment of one hundred men and officers from the 6th, 19th, and 28th Ga. Vols. A false alarm was created by the report of a blue light. The men got upon the ramparts in fair time, with only a moderate amount of skulking.

FORT SUMTER, November 12, 1863.

Number of shells fired yesterday was: from rifled guns, twenty-three (23), of which thirteen (13) missed; from mortars, one hundred and ninety-six (196), of which one hundred and thirteen (113) missed. During the night one hundred and forty-six (146) rifled shots were fired, of which thirty-three missed, and eight (8) mortar shells, of which five missed.

First Sergeant Wayles Langford, Co. "G," 1st S. C. Art'y, was wounded in the head slightly by a piece of shell while his company was on the parapet.

At 8 P.M. a calcium light was displayed at Gregg, for the apparent purpose of illuminating our works, and preventing the location of obstructions upon the slopes.

At 9 P. M. rapid musketry firing was observed at Gregg, while voices were heard to cry out "Halt." The occasion has not been discovered.

At 11 P. M. Co. "G," 1st Regt. S. C. A., Captain W. H. Perronneau, forty (40) men, was relieved by Co. "D," 1st Regt. S. C. A., Captain Harleston, forty-five (45) men: Owing to the refusal of the captain of the steamer to approach the fort, the final transfer was made on board of small boats, and consumed much time.

The flagstaff was shot down, and the flag was replaced by Sergeant Mayo, Co. " B," and Private Robert Aubry, Co. "C," 28th Ga. Vols.

FORT SUMTER, November 13, 1863.

Firing yesterday: Rifled shots, one hundred and forty-four, of which thirty-four missed; mortars, one hundred and fifty-nine, of which ninety-two missed; monitors fired twice, struck both times; one shot passed through the flag. During the night one hundred and eighty rifles fired, of which fifty-one passed over; monitors, two hundred and eighty-two, of which one hundred and ten missed.

The following casualties occurred: Private W. J. Hadden, Co. "I," 28th Ga., killed by a fragment of Parrott shell while on post; Private A. J. Clinton, Co. "K," 17th S. C. V., killed by a mortar shell while on post: Private E. Johnson, Co. "C," 25th S. C. V. wounded severely in face while on post. A strong light was thrown from Fort Gregg upon the fort during a greater part of the night.

Major Pringle effected a transfer of negroes and a transportation of commissary stores in small boats without loss, assisted by Lieutenant Swinton, under a very heavy fire.

FORT SUMTER, November 14, 1863.

Shots fired yesterday: Rifled, fired seventy-four, of which nine missed; mortars, three hundred and fifteen, of which one hundred and twenty-eight missed. During the night: Rifles, one hundred and fifteen, of which thirty-six missed. To-day there were twenty-one rifle shots fired, of which nine missed. Mortars fired two hundred and twenty-five, of which ninety-six missed. Private J. G. Pound, Co. "K," 27th Ga., was dangerously wounded in the thigh by a fragment of a mortar shell. A boat was seen lying at the obstructions last night. When hailed, she proved to be our guard boat; her presence there does not contribute to the safety of this work.

FORT SUMTER, November 15, 1863.

Shelling continued heavy last night. Ninety-eight (98) rifled shells were fired, of which thirty-nine (39) missed, and two hundred and nineteen (219) mortar shells were thrown, of which ninety (90) missed. Casualties were as follows: Private J. R. Wilson, Co. "K," 27th Ga., shoulder, slight; N. P. Benton, Co. "A," 27th Ga., scalp, slight; William Ment, Co. "H," 27th Ga., back, slight.

To-day rifles, fired sixteen (16), of which six (6) missed; mortar shells, three hundred and twenty (320), of which one hundred and fifteen (115) missed. Casualties to-day: First Sergeant J. C. Grimball, Co. "D," 1st Regiment S. C. Artillery, wounded severely in head, abdomen, and knee, by a mortar shell. I append a statement of the Engineers' work as furnished by Captain Johnson: Nov. 14th, 15th. Repaired top of traverse over three-gun battery; construction of Inf. epaulment, west front, near south-west pan-coupé; built barricade, with loopholes at north end of three-gun battery; began remodelling east end of centre bomb-proof for infantry defence.

Obstructions repaired, placed, and taken in.

FORT SUMTER, November 16, 1863.

Enemy fired last night one hundred and eighty-four rifled shots, of which fifty-two (52) missed, and twelve mortar shells, of which two (2) missed. To-day forty-three (43) rifled shots were fired, of which five (5) missed, and three hundred and sixty-three (363) mortar shells, of which one hundred and eighteen (118) missed. Number of shots of all kinds fired during the past week up to this morning, three thousand and thirty. This morning four monitors took position near the Cumings Point buoy. Two pairs of buoys were discharged by them on the flood tide; they passed up the channel between the obstructions and Fort Sumter. I am led to believe that they carried heavy weights suspended at a certain depth below the surface of the water, and were designed to prove whether there was a practical passage for vessels of a certain draught.

FORT SUMTER, November 17, 1863.

Enemy fired last night as follows: Rifled shots, one hundred and fifty-six, of which fifty-five missed; mortar shells six, one of which missed. To-day fourteen rifle shots were fired, of which five missed, and three hundred and sixty-six mortar shells, of which one hundred and seventeen missed. Last night Private Edmund Lake, Co. "D," 27th S. C. V., acting coxswain of the quartermaster's boat, was killed by a fragment of shell while approaching the fort. No casualties to-day.

FORT SUMTER, November 18, 1863.

Enemy fired last night as follows: Rifle shots, one hundred and thirty-three (133), eleven (11) of which missed. To-day twelve (12) rifle shots were fired, of which four (4) missed, and two hundred and seventy-eight (278) mortar shells; of these ninety-two (92) missed. At about 1:30 o'clock, the sentinel at the northeast angle descried a small boat approaching the fort; he hailed it several times, and was answered with an oath; he thereupon fired, and the boat immediately retreated. A short time afterwards there was considerable musketry firing directed towards the fort, apparently from boats between this fort and Gregg. Several balls struck the fort, and some passed over.

Later, near daylight, two boats approached within four hundred yards, opposite the southeast angle; they were fired upon and retreated towards Morris Island. No casualties since my last report.

I append a brief statement of engineer work done last night. The force (one hundred and twenty) worked on repairs of southwest angle bomb-proof over stair, constructing position for howitzer at west sally-port casemate, filling ordnance storeroom, southwest angle, and completing loopholed blindage east and centre bomb-proof. Garrison worked on filling passage to southeast magazine.

FORT SUMTER, November 19, 1863.

Two hundred and eighty-five (285) rifle shots were fired last night, of which ninety-six (96) missed, and three (3) mortar shell which struck. To-day forty-four (44) rifle shots were fired, of which nine (9) missed, and three hundred and sixty-two (362) mortar shells, of which one hundred and thirteen (113) missed. No casualties have occurred since the last report.

Engineer in charge reports that his working force was engaged during the night repairing large holes over centre bomb-proof, also filling ordnance storeroom adjoining western magazine, second tier.

Completed loopholes in splinter-proof at east end of centre bomb-proof, and continued filling passages inside south angle, and blew up middle kitchen in east barracks.

Captain Mitchell, with three (3) officers and one hundred (100) men from 6th, 19th, 23d, and 27th Georgia Regiments, relieved Captain Rentfro with three (3) officers and one hundred (100) men from the 6th, 27th, and 28th Georgia.

Rifles, fired to-day forty-four (44), nine (9) missed. Mortars, three hundred and sixty-two (362), one hundred and thirteen (113) missed. No casualties.

[*By Telegraph.*]

12:35 P. M.—Give my respects to the Colonel Commanding, and say that we are in fine health and good spirits to-day at being in communication with the outer world once more.

FORT SUMTER, November 20, 1863.

Rifles, fired last night ninety-seven (97), of which twenty-five (25) missed. At half-past two, the moon being down and the weather very favorable for an attack, I aroused and placed the whole garrison under arms. Before visiting Captain Harleston's quarters, I found that he had taken the same precautions. At three o'clock a detachment of the enemy's barges, variously estimated at from four to nine in number, approached within three hundred yards of the fort and opened fire with musketry.

Most of the troops got into position very rapidly, but in spite of all instructions commenced a random fire, into the air on the part of many, at the distant boats on the part of others. The troops stationed in the centre bomb-proof, for the most part refused to ascend the parapet, though encouraged by the example of Lieutenant Mironell and a few other brave men.

I have sent a despatch to General Taliaferro, asking him to relieve two lieutenants who did not behave well. I have not evidence enough to convict them, but do not want them here longer. I have taken measures which I trust may ensure better conduct in the future.

No rockets were sent up because positive attacks were not made. The ricochet practice from Sullivan's Island was very handsome. The fire from Johnson was very bad, the balls passing directly over the fort.

Private T. Whester, Company "D," 1st South Carolina Artillery, was wounded slightly in the head yesterday by a brick.

I respectfully request that, if practicable, Captain Harleston be retained here until the dark nights have entirely passed by. His removal just at this time will be a great misfortune to me, as I am greatly dependent on his watchfulness and ability.

Report of Engineer in charge.

Major W. H. ECHOLS, *Chief-Engineer So. Ca.*

MAJOR,—I have the honor to report the firing last night was as follows: Rifle shots ninety-seven, of which twenty-five missed. The working force was engaged upon filling passages to east magazine and casemate, preparing two casemates over hospital for loop-holed musketry defence, and repairing top of central bomb-proof.

The working force of one hundred and thirty, under overseer McNeill, was relieved by fresh force of one hundred and nineteen, under overseer Mickle. The transfer occupied about one hour, and was effected without any casualty.

At 3 A. M. musketry firing from the parapets creating an alarm, the force was withdrawn. Three or four boats from the enemy had been discovered on the sea front, and when fired on were seen to return the fire. The James Island and Sullivan Island batteries opened in our support, also the gunboat off Fort Johnson. The alarm subsided in an hour. During the night two slight casualties. The enemy's light was shown during the alarm, but their fire was suspended a half hour.

The firing to-day was heavy and as follows: Rifles, eighteen, of which eight missed.

Mortars, three hundred and seventy-nine, of which one hundred and forty-six missed.

Total three hundred and ninety-seven, of which one hundred and fifty-four missed.

About 10:30 A. M. a mortar shell descending at entrance to east end of centre bomb-proof, cut through without much smashing the timber blindage just erected, and exploding wounded severely one of my carpenters, and slightly another, while a third man of the garrison was mortally wounded and is since dead.

The extra mortar firing is due to the new mortars reported by me yesterday. I would respectfully suggest the propriety of shelling them from Battery Simkins, as they are favorably situated on that side of Gregg.

Respectfully submitted,
(Signed,) JOHN JOHNSON,
Captain Eng'rs.

DEFENCE OF FORT SUMTER. 143

[*By Telegraph.*]

9:45 A. M. Enemy shelling us more heavily this morning than usual with mortars. Have fired few rifled shots. I will send up report of last night's proceedings after a while.

Rifle shots, fired eighteen (18); missed ten (10). Mortars, fired three hundred and seventy-seven (377); missed one hundred and forty-six (146). One man killed.

FORT SUMTER, November 21, 1863.

Last night one hundred and twenty-four (124) rifle shots were fired, of which forty-one (41) passed over without exploding.

At 9 P. M. Captain Burley, 17th S. C. V., and Lieutenant Hutchinson, 6th Ga., relieved Lieutenants Coleman and James, of the same regiments, respectively, who were removed at my request. Thomas Hornbuckle, Co. "C," 28d Ga., was killed yesterday by the explosion of a mortar shell; wounded: C. Banks, Co. "K," 17th S. C. V., spine, slight; W. R. Brown, private, Matthewes Art'y, shoulder, severe; Alexander Stewart, Co. "B," 6th Ga., scalp, slight. At 5 A. M. the broken arch on the gorge wall was struck by a Parrott shell and fell, killing two (2) negroes, and wounding six (6), and wounding Private Charles Etheridge, Co. "H," 6th Ga., fractured jaw, and Coote Thayer, Co. "H," 6th Ga., spine, slight: repeated efforts had been made a few hours before to pull it down, but to no purpose. The following is a statement of the Engineer work done last night, as submitted by Captain Johnson: Filled and loopholed two arches over magazine, completed filling passage in south angle, repaired tops of battery and central bomb-proof. Began covering with sand bags the loopholed blindage, east end corner bomb-proof.

[*By Telegraph.*]

7:40.—Rifle shots fired to-day twenty-three (23), seven (7) of which missed. Mortars, two hundred and thirty-eight (238), ninety-nine (99) of which missed.

FORT SUMTER, November 22, 1863.

At night one hundred and forty-nine (149) rifled shells were fired, forty-five (45) of them exploded after passing the fort. There have been no casualties, neither has any serious damage been done to the work. At three (3) A. M. this morning a blue light was reported at the entrance to Vincent's Creek; the parapet was handsomely manned by the garrison. No further indication of the enemy's advance appears.

[*By Telegraph.*]

Rifled shots to-day four (4). Mortars, one hundred and forty-three (143), of which sixty-three (63) missed. Bomb-proof was whitewashed by Captain Johnson a week ago.

2:30 P. M.—I have sixty-five (65) double-barrel shot guns.

FORT SUMTER, November 23, 1863.

Last night ninety-four (94) rifle shots were fired, of which twenty-four (24) missed. Captain Hopkins and six (6) officers and one hundred and eight (108) men from the 27th S. C. Volunteers, relieved Captain Crawford, 17th S. C. Volunteers, ten (10) officers, and one hundred and one (101) men. No casualties.

[*By Telegraph.*]

Rifled, seven (7); none missed. Mortars, one hundred and ninety-two (192), of which eighty-one (81) missed. No loss.

FORT SUMTER, November 24, 1863.

During the night one hundred and seventy (170) rifle shells were fired, of which sixty-two (62) exploded after passing, or passed without bursting. It is my painful duty to report that Captain F. H Harleston, Co. "D," 1st S. C. Art'y, was wounded in both thighs and in the arm by a Parrott shell, at half-past four. He had gone down the slope of the sea-face to examine the obstructions which had been reported as being washed away by the tide. He is mortally hurt. One negro was killed, and another lost his leg by fragments of Parrott shells.

Captain Harleston is sinking; he is under the influence of anodyne. He bore his sufferings most manfully, and was averse to taking any opiates, which it became necessary to administer on account of his great pain. His whole anxiety seemed to be on account of his mother. He was perfectly calm, and as cheerful as his great sufferings would permit. Lieutenant-Colonel Cock has received some messages from him to his relatives.

The enemy firing upon Sumter with mortars. Occasionally upon Moultrie and Simkins and Johnson with guns. No damage of consequence yesterday or last night. Negroes are working briskly on Gregg. The 300-pounder at middle battery is turned upon Moultrie.

Rifles fired, two (2), and both missed; mortar shells, ninety-eight (98), of which thirty-three (33) missed. No casualties.

Captain Harleston died at a quarter-past ten (10:15) o'clock this morning.

FORT SUMTER, November 25, 1863.

Our report for last night is: Rifled, fired one hundred and sixty-six (166), of which one hundred and fifteen (115) struck; mortar shell, fired seventeen (17), only six (6) of which struck. The casualties last night were: Captain Mitchell, Co. " F," 23d Ga., slightly wounded, one negro killed, and another severely wounded in shoulder.

FORT SUMTER, November 26, 1863.

Ten rifle shell were thrown yesterday at the fort, of which three missed, and eleven mortar shells, of which three also missed. During the night two hundred and forty-two (242) rifle shell were fired, of which eighty-eight (88) missed. There have been no casualties nor any material injury done to the work since last report.

Rifles fired to-day twenty-three (23), five of which missed; mortars, forty-eight (48), eighteen (18) of which missed. No casualties.

FORT SUMTER, November 27, 1863.

Last night one hundred and sixty-nine rifled shell were thrown, of which ninety-two missed. There have been no casualties during the last twenty-four hours, neither has the injury to the work been serious. Captain Roe with a detachment of one hundred men from the 19th, 23d, 27th, and 28th Ga., were relieved by Captain Jordan with six officers and one hundred (100) men from the same regiments.

The following statement of work done is submitted by the Engineer:

Continued and nearly completed extension of traverse over loop-holed blindage at entrance of battery. Blocked up western sally-port within and without; continued and nearly completed filling of ordnance storeroom, second tier, west pan-coupé; completed barrier of sand bags at north end of hospital casemates; completed machicoule gallery over northwest beam; continued mining for passages from centre bomb-proof through lower gorge rooms towards south magazines.

FORT SUMTER, November 28, 1863.

Enemy fired one hundred and six (106) shots yesterday from the land batteries, fifty-three (53) of which missed, and one hundred and five (105) mortar shell, forty (40) of which missed. The westernmost of the two heavy guns at Gregg bearing upon this point is ascertained to be a 10-inch Columbiad. The shell practice of this gun at the southwest angle was very good, and rather effective. Fragments of a 13-inch mortar shell were also found yesterday. During the night the usual practice with light Parrotts continued; fired two hundred and fifty-seven (257), missed one hundred and thirty-six (136). Private James Tupper, Jr., shot-marker, Company "D," 27th S. C. V. (Charleston Battalion), seeing yesterday morning that the flag had been shot down, walked along the whole extent of the gorge wall on the parapet and endeavored to raise it; finding that the staff was too short, he procured an additional piece of spar and with the assistance of C. B. Foster, same command, and Corporal W. C. Buckheister and A. J. Bluett, Company "B," same corps, succeeded in splicing and planting the staff under a very heavy fire directed at them. One shot cut the flag from their hands. It was a most distinguished display of gallantry.

No casualties have occurred since last report.

FORT SUMTER, November 29, 1863.

Land guns fired yesterday ninety-seven (97) shots, of which forty-three (43) missed, mortars fired twenty-one (21), of which six (6) missed, and a monitor, twenty-two (22), of which eight (8) missed. Last night one hundred and twenty-six (126) shots were fired, of which fifty-nine (59) missed; one mortar shell, which struck. No boats arrived from the city last night. No casualties occurred.

Rifled, fired to-day one hundred and seven (107), of which fifty (50) missed; mortars, one hundred and five (105), of which forty (40) missed; Columbiads, fifteen (15), of which three (3) missed. No casualties.

Rifled, fired to-day eight (8), of which four (4) missed.

FORT SUMTER, November 30, 1863.

Last night one hundred and forty (140) rifle shots were fired, seventy-four (74) of which missed, and four mortar shells, all of which fell outside. A negro was killed by a Parrott shell last night. A good deal of signalling was observed during the night on board the fleet, on Morris Island, and on Black Island. The Engineer workdone consisted of uncovering and reconstructing bomb-proof over southwest stairway, extending mining galleries towards east magazine from centre bomb-proof, and from northwest casemates to battery. No bags of sand arrived last two nights, weather preventing.

Number of rifled shots fired, one—struck; mortars, fired twenty-two (22), of which eleven (11) missed. No casualties.

FORT SUMTER, December 1, 1863.

Enemy fired yesterday, rifled, one—struck; mortars, twenty-two, of which eleven missed. Last night twenty-two mortar shells were fired, of which eleven missed. No damage; no casualties.

Eight (8) mortars, of which four (4) missed.

FORT SUMTER, December 2, 1863.

Fire on this place almost totally ceased. Six (6) mortar shells were thrown yesterday, of which two (2) missed.

No firing last night.

A detachment of six (6) officers and one hundred (100) men from 19th, 6th, 27th, and 28th Ga. Volunteers, under Captain Bateman, relieved detachment of three (3) officers and one hundred (100) men, under Captain Mitchell, from 19th, 27th, 23d, and 28th Ga. Volunteers.

FORT SUMTER, December 3, 1863.

Enemy reopened fire yesterday at half-past ten (10:30), throwing seventy-two (72) rifle shots, of which twenty-six (26) missed; seventy-three (73) mortar shells, of which thirty-eight (38) missed, and sixty-eight (68) Columbiad shot and shell, of which fourteen (14) missed. There was no firing last night. James Fowler, private, Co. "H," 27th S. C. Volunteers, wounded by shell in head slightly.

FORT SUMTER, December 4, 1863.

Fire of the enemy commenced yesterday at one o'clock at the southwest angle. Twenty-seven (27) Columbiad shots were thrown, of which one (1) missed, and eleven (11) rifled, of which two (2) missed. Damage inflicted not considerable. I have made a careful examination of the exterior of the fort this morning. The slope is exceedingly steep and the footing very insecure. Nothing like a rush can ever be made up these slopes as long as they retain their present inclination.

FORT SUMTER, December 5, 1863.

Forty-two (42) rifled shot were fired yesterday, of which eleven (11) missed; Columbiads, thirty-five (35), of which ten (10) missed, and seventeen (17) mortars, of which nine (9) missed. Last night forty-nine (49) rifled were fired, of which twenty-seven (27) missed; Columbiads, six (6) fired, of which two (2) missed. Captain Sellers, with three (3) officers and eighty-nine (89) men, relieved Captain Hopkins, six (6) officers and one hundred and seven (107) men.

Number of shots fired to-day, six rifle, of which two missed. No casualties.

FORT SUMTER, December 8, 1863.

No shots have been fired at this fort since the last morning report. The enemy are at work revetting the batteries, and appear to be extending Gregg to the eastward. Wagons could be seen moving down the beach towards Wagner yesterday afternoon.

At dusk, parties of two or three hundred men could be seen moving down towards Gregg. The pitching of one of the monitors yesterday revealed some timber work at the boat, whose exact nature the strength of my glass did not permit me to make out.

I do not think it is well for our batteries to suspend their fire when the enemy are silent, as they are working when not firing. They are then more exposed and vulnerable.

FORT SUMTER, December 9, 1863.

Affairs here continue quiet. The enemy show themselves in considerable numbers at Gregg and Wagner, where the work of cutting, hauling, and placing sods continues. A large steam transport, a schooner, and a gunboat have been seen to go by to the southward this morning.

Six (6) rifled shots were fired to-day, of which one (1) missed.

FORT SUMTER, December 10, 1863.

Enemy fired six (6) light rifle shots yesterday, all of which struck except one. Captain Harkey, with six (6) officers and one hundred (100) men from the 6th, 19th, 23d, and 27th Ga., relieved Captain Jordan, six (6) officers and one hundred (100) men, from the 19th, 23d, 27th, and 28th Ga. Enemy continued working, but are seriously interrupted by our shelling when it takes place.

One rifled shot fired to-day, and missed.

FORT SUMTER, December 11, 1863.

Captain Gaillard, Co. "K," 1st S. C. Art'y, forty (40) men relieved Captain Peronneau, Co. "G," forty (40) men; same corps last night.

There was no firing yesterday, nor any unusual movements on Morris Island.

[*By Telegraph.*]

4:40 o'clock.—Small-arm magazine exploded. Send provisions, one hundred (100) muskets, buckshot cartridges, and fifty (50) men; also set of telegraph instruments and two hundred yards of wire.

FORT JOHNSTON, December 11, 9:15 P. M.

The Colonel is here; has ordered one hundred (100) men of the reserve stationed here to go to Fort Sumter. Have necessary orders from General Beauregard sent down to Colonel Harrison.

Steamer will be at Southern Wharf in three (3) hours; have a fire engine ready to go to Fort Sumter.

Have also as many of the following articles ready as soon as possible to send down: Torch and turpentine for Signal Corps; a signal officer ordered down; hand-grenades; one hundred rounds of howitzer ammunition; five thousand (5,000) musket cartridges; two hundred (200) muskets; thirty (30) days' rations and a commissary officer.

A hand-saw, cross-cut saw, two cross-cut saw files, two hundred yards submarine cable; set of instruments for telegraph, and lead pencil and writing paper for telegraph operator.

Forty (40) men were killed and wounded by the explosion of small-arms ammunition; Captain Frost, A. C. S., among the killed; Lieutenant-Colonel Elliott slightly wounded; three of Gaillard's men killed and two wounded; among the killed is Sergeant Swanston; only three bodies of killed have been recovered. The casemates of west face and southwest of pan-coupé are still burning. Have ambulances at Southern Wharf for the wounded; send Colonel Rhett's and my horses to Southern Wharf at once.

(Signed,)   IREDELL JONES,
    A. A. D. C.

To Lieutenant S. C. BOYLSTON,
    A. A. A. G.

SIGNAL STATION, December 11, 1863.

To General THOMAS JORDAN, *Chief of Staff.*

The following message was sent to Colonel Harrison at Fort Johnson, and which we are instructed by Colonel Rhett to forward to you:

"Small-arm magazine exploded; send provisions, one hundred

(100) muskets, buckshot cartridges, fifty (50) men; also a set of telegraph instruments, and two hundred (200) yards of wire."

The above is from Colonel Elliott, commanding Fort Sumter. Can you send the men from Fort Johnson? If so, let me know at once.

(Signed,) Lieutenant BOYLSTON,
A. A. A. G.

FORT SUMTER, December 11, 1863.

To Lieutenant BOYLSTON, A. A. A. G.

LIEUTENANT,—Lieutenant-Colonel Elliott being slightly wounded, and having placed me temporarily in command of the fort, I would respectfully beg leave to submit the following report of shots fired at the fort to-day:

```
Rifled shots, hit........................125
   "      missed......................  18
                                        ———
Total rifled fired........................143

Mortar shells, hit......................  62
   "      missed......................  15
                                        ———
Total shots and shells fired...............220
```

The Signal Corps established communication this evening, but cannot to-night.

FORT SUMTER, December, 12, 1863.

At 9:30 yesterday morning the southwest magazine exploded. Owing to a want of space, the ammunition for small arms and howitzers, amounting to about one hundred and fifty pounds of powder, was stored in the inner room. The commissary stores were kept principally in the outer room, which was also used as an issuing office. The material in these rooms were immediately ignited, their occupants killed, and those stationed in the adjoining passages either killed or burnt with greater or less severity.

The passages leading to the lower and upper tiers of casemates, and those casemates themselves, were filled constantly with the most dense smoke, introduced by a blast of great strength, whose flame was visible from the room occupied as headquarters. In total darkness the occupants rushed from the stifling smoke to the open embrasures, leaving their arms and blankets behind.

The continuance of the smoke prevented any prolonged attempt to obstruct the progress of the fire. With great promptness a boat was sent from the navy with a supply of water buckets.

The telegraph apparatus was removed and located at another position, by Mr. W. R. Cathcart, the operator, who behaved remarkably well, but he was compelled to retire from this second position by the advance of the fire.

The signal officers made repeated efforts to attract the attention of Sullivan's Island and Fort Johnson, but were unable to succeed till a late hour in the day. The Sullivan's Island corps could be seen operating with other points, and inattention, when it was known that we were under unusual circumstances, and cut off from all communication, seems to me reprehensible in the extreme, and ought, I think, to be looked into.

The effect of the fire was to destroy the roof of the magazine and the southwest stairway, the woodwork in the two tiers of casemates as far, in the lower, as the old sally-port.

The damage done will not materially affect the defence of the work. Captain Johnson, of the Engineers, was everywhere, doing everything that man could do.

Lieutenant Harper, Co. "F," 25th S. C. V., showed great gallantry in rescuing burning bodies from the smoke and flames. Captain Sellers, of the same company, gave me great assistance in superintending the arrangements last night, at a time when a slight temporary injury prevented me from running about.

Soon after the fire became apparent the enemy opened fire, throwing one hundred and forty-three rifle shots, of which eighteen missed, and seventy-seven mortar shells, of which fifteen missed. The deficiencies in men, arms, ammunition, and commissary stores, were most promptly supplied by the authorities.

The following is a list of the casualties:

Killed.—Captain Edward Frost, N. C. S.; Sergeant Hammond, White's Battalion Art'y; Sergeant John King, Co. "E," 25th S. C. V.; Thomas McElwyn, Co. "E," 25th S. C. V.; B. Douglas, Co. "F," 25th S. C. V.; Sergeant Robert Swanston, Co. "K," 1st S. C. Art'y; P. Sill, Co. "K," 1st S. C. Art'y; A. Surten, Co. "K," 1st S. C. Art'y; W. J. Lee, Co. "I," 19th Ga.; B. Jones, Co. "H," 19th Ga.; J. T. Ford, Co. "G," 27th Ga.

Wounded.—Lieutenant-Colonel Elliott, slight, in head and ankle; Captain Mazyck, Co. "E," 25th S. C. V.; C. F. Voehler, Co. "E," 25th S. C. V.; J. Brenard, Co. "E," 25th S. C. V.; Sergeant J. E.

Prince, Co. "E," 25th S. C. V.; R. Flotwell, Co. "E," 25th S. C. V.; T. Callaghan, Co. "E," 25th S. C. V.; H. Hutson, Co. "E;" D. H. Clayton, Co. "E;" C. Festic, Co. "F;" D. Avinger, Co. "F."

Privates C. Speigner, Co. "F," 25th S. C. V.; N. W. Shuler, Co. "F," S. C. V.; P. H. Taylor, Co. "F," 25th S. C. V.; R. D. Zimmerman, Co. "F," 25th S. C. V.; W. C. Zimmerman, Co. "F," 25th S. C. V.; H. Shier, Co. "F," 25th S. C. V.; B. Buhn, Co. "B," 19th Ga. Vols.; N. C. Jones, Co. "H," 19th Ga. Vols.; Elisha Harris, Company "E," 6th Ga. Vols.; J. B. Buckman, Co. "G," 19th Ga. Vols.; B. P. Brooks, Co. "G," 6th Ga. Vols.; J. M. Huddleston, Co. "E," 19th Ga. Vols.; W. Dunning, Co. "H," 27th Ga. Vols.; N. F. Smith, Co. "C," 19th Ga. Vols.; J. Hemphill, Co. "C," 27th Ga. Vols.; H. W. Wells, Co. "E," 6th Ga. Vols.; J. Hodge, Co. "A," 27th Ga. Vols.; J. S. Price, Co. "C," 6th Ga. Vols.; W. B. Chandler, Co. "K," 6th Ga. Vols.; W. B. Leatherwood, Co. "I," 19th Ga. Vols.; H. C. Adair, Co. "H," 19th Ga. Vols.; J. M. Carney, Co. "A," 6th Ga. Vols.; Sergeant Reed, Co. "K," 19th Ga. Vols.; Private W. F. Dannan, Co. "A," 27th Ga. Vols.; Sergeant J. C. Calhoun, Co. "A," 27th Ga. Vols.; Privates L. Mashburn, Co. "K," 1st S. C. Art'y; J. Leech, Co. "K," 1st S. C. Art'y; L. W. Dantyler, Co. "F," 25th S. C. Vols.; Percival Elliott, Signal Corps; B. D. Watson, Co. "D," 6th Ga. Vols.

Recapitulation.

Killed 11
Wounded 41
Total 52

FORT SUMTER, December 12, 1863.

Captain OTEY:

I will send back the thirty-second (32d) Georgia troops, as I can spare them.

FORT SUMTER, December 13, 1863.

Brigadier-General THOMAS JORDAN, *Chief of Staff:*

Communication with Fort Sumter resumed at four (4) o'clock this A. M.

Very respectfully,
(Signed,) J. W. KATES,
Superintendent.

FORT SUMTER, December 13, 1863.

The steamer did not communicate last night, her commander alleging as a reason the heavy weather, which was, however, not bad enough to prevent the passage of the guard and telegraph boats.

During the middle and latter portions of the night the wind subsided, and a more passable opportunity could not have been obtained. I am surprised that movements of importance should be left to the discretion and final decision of irresponsible and timid steamboat captains.

The passage can be made with little risk, by running down on the Sullivan's Island side until the light is shut in, and then turning for the fort, and keeping in its shades until the wharf is reached.

I sent by the guard-boat last night the report of yesterday morning and the day before.

The passages are cooling slowly. The gorge wall is much sunken in over the exploded magazine.

We have no rations for to-morrow. No fire-engine has come. I would like the garrison reduced to the original number to-night, if convenient.

The action of the waves has made the slopes inaccessible at present, though at the loss of much valuable material. No firing yesterday.

[*By Telegraph.*]

4:40 P. M.—The fire has burnt out, except in ruins of the magazine. I do not think it can spread any further. The northwest casemates are gradually cooling off.

FORT SUMTER, December 14, 1863.

Captain Abercrombie with six (6) officers and one hundred (100) men from 6th, 19th, 27th, and 23d Ga. Regiments, relieved Captain Bateman, six (6) officers, and one hundred (100) men, from 6th, 19th, 27th, and 28th Regiments.

The steamer effected a landing last night, with a supply of ordnance and commissary stores. Casemates cooling.

FORT SUMTER, December 15, 1863.

I have the honor to report a day of extreme quiet yesterday. Details from the garrison were assigned to the Engineer, for the purpose of assisting in the removal of rubbish.

The work of repair goes on well.

FORT SUMTER, December 16, 1863.

Captain Franklin with six (6) officers and one hundred (100) men, from the 6th, 23d, 27th, and 28th Ga. Regiments, relieved Captain Harkery with six (6) officers and one hundred (100) men, from 6th, 19th, 23d, and 27th. Affairs continue quiet. The repair of the damage progressing.

Transportation and water were supplied.

FORT SUMTER, December 17, 1863.

Captain R. Chisolm with six (6) officers and one hundred (100) men, from the 27th Regiment S. C. V., relieved Captain Sellers with six (6) officers and eighty-three (83) men, 25th Regiment S. C. V. Private Laith, Gist Guard, reported as ordnance sergeant one week after the receipt of my copy of the order providing for his attachment.

FORT SUMTER, December 18, 1863.

I have the honor to enclose my morning report of yesterday, which, owing to my absence in the city, was not made out. I beg leave to report, that on my return to my post yesterday evening, I found Captain Johnson of the Engineers with a high fever, and as there were no comforts here, recommended his removal to the city until he shall have recovered. Mr. Delisle and Mr. Hall, assistant engineers, are carrying on the work. I penetrated this morning to the portion of the magazine used a commissary store house. A small amount of burning material is on the floor, but by the use of buckets the fire will soon be totally extinguished. The work of revetting and obstructing the approach to the works on Morris Island is still going forward.

FORT SUMTER, December 19, 1863.

I have the honor to report that we have still been unmolested by the enemy, and that the Engineer work has progressed as favorably as usual.

FORT SUMTER December 20, 1863.

I have the honor to report that nothing unusual occurred on yesterday. The monitors were actively moving about this morning, but soon resumed their anchorage.

FORT SUMTER, December 21, 1863.

I have the honor to report that affairs continue the same at this post. Enemy busily engaged in turfing slopes at Wagner and in extending the flanks of Gregg. The latter is mostly done at night. Our shelling has but little effect on them. I would respectfully recommend to the Commanding General that some system of observation and correction of our mortar practice be adopted.

FORT SUMTER, December 22, 1863.

I have the honor to report that last night Captain Butts of the 23d Ga. Regiment, with six (6) officers and one hundred and nine (109) enlisted men from the 19th, 23d, 27th, and 28th Ga., relieved Captain Abercrombie of the same regiment, and six (6) officers with one hundred and one (101) enlisted men from the 6th, 23d, 27th and 19th Ga.; also that last night about one o'clock one of the enemy's barges appeared off the fort and continued sounding for some time; it finally retired towards Morris Island.

The condition of the fort is very much the same as usual, all changes being for the better.

FORT SUMTER, December 23, 1863.

I have the honor to report quiet this morning.

The fleet consists of the "Ironsides," four monitors, one mortar boat, three wooden gunboats, and fourteen sailing vessels inside; four blockaders outside, and sixteen craft in Lighthouse Inlet.

Gregg is undergoing some change, but its nature is not sufficiently developed to report upon.

In correction of yesterday's report, I have the honor to state that the barge was reported as taking soundings. I am not certain that she was actually engaged in that work.

FORT SUMTER, December 24, 1863.

I have the honor to report in sight the "Ironsides," four (4) monitors, four (4) gunboats, two (2) mortar boats, one of which was concealed yesterday, three (3) tugs, and fifteen (15) sailing vessels inside. Four blockaders, one tug, and one schooner outside, and twenty vessels and steamers in Lighthouse Inlet. Discrepancies in morning reports may arise from changes in the grouping of the vessels; in some cases an accurate estimate is very difficult. One, and sometimes two monitors come upon picket duty at night within fourteen hundred (1,400) yards of the fort. No perceptible change on Morris Island. Captain Johnson reported for duty last night.

FORT SUMTER, December 25, 1863.

I have the honor to report the "Ironsides," four monitors, three wooden gunboats, two mortar boats, one tug, and fourteen sailing vessels inside this morning. Four blockaders and eighteen vessels in Lighthouse Inlet. Heavy firing at daylight and several hours afterwards in direction of Stono. Detachment of six officers and one hundred men from 6th, 23d, 27th, and 28th Ga. Regiments, under Captain Morse, relieved Captain Douglas, six officers, and one hundred men from 6th, 23d, 27th, and 28th Ga. Regiments. The accidental explosion of an old shell wounded Privates Theodore Yeault and Joseph Lee, Co. "K," 1st S. C. Art'y, slightly.

FORT SUMTER, December 26, 1863.

"Ironsides," four (4) monitors, two (2) mortar boats, two (2) wooden gunboats, four (4) tugs, and (15) sailing vessels inside. Four blockaders and eighteen vessels in Lighthouse Inlet.

At twelve (12) yesterday, at the signals of a steam whistle from the fleet and a gun from the direction of Lighthouse Inlet, the enemy raised a flag on the middle battery. It may be a significant fact that at the first attempt the bunting went up union down.

FORT SUMTER, December 27, 1863.

* * The embrasure formerly occupied by the 10-inch Columbiad at Gregg is closed up. The large Parrott is the only heavy gun bearing on us from that point. No embrasure is so extended as to embrace a very large field of fire. No working parties have been observed on Morris Island during the last few days.

FORT SUMTER, December 28, 1863.

I have the honor to report that I have been unable to make a correct estimation of the fleet this morning. Observations yesterday showed only one light gun at Gregg bearing on this point, where there were four previously.

Captain King, forty-one men, Co. "D," 1st S. C. Art'y, relieved Captain Gaillard, Co. "K," thirty-five men, last night. There was a good deal of signalling last night between the fleet and Morris Island.

FORT SUMTER, December 29, 1863.

"Ironsides," four monitors, four wooden gunboats, fifteen sailing vessels, and two mortar-boats inside. Four blockaders, four sailing vessels, and two tugs outside. Fifteen vessels in Lighthouse Inlet; one large and three small Parrotts in position at Gregg.

FORT SUMTER, December 30, 1863.

I have the honor to call your attention to the fact that Companies "G" and "H," 25th S. C. V., and Co. "D," 1st S. C. Art'y, are the only companies at this post sufficiently entire to admit of their being mustered here. I therefore respectfully recommend that instructions be sent to the regiments of General Colquitt's Brigade, and to the remainder of the 25th S. C. V., to have the names of these members of their respective organizations now on duty at this post, enrolled upon the muster rolls made out at regimental headquarters; the men can be accounted for in the remarks, and my post return will give the strength and composition of the garrison.

In sight this morning the "Ironsides," four monitors, three wooden gunboats, two mortar boats, and sixteen sailing vessels, and two tugs inside; three blockaders and one schooner outside, and fifteen craft in Lighthouse Inlet. The embrasure at the 10-inch Columbiad at Gregg, is being reopened. Captain Hammond, six officers, one hundred men from 25th S. C. V., relieved Captain Chisolm and force from 27th S. C. V., last night.

FORT SUMTER, December 31, 1863.

I have the honor to report that there were indications of some parade of ceremony on Morris Island yesterday afternoon. Music was heard, batteries fired their guns, the slopes of the works at the southern end of the Island were thronged with men, and a steamer with more than the usual amount of decorations lay at the landing at Lighthouse Inlet. A volley of musketry was also heard at 8 P. M.

FORT SUMTER, January 1, 1864.

I have the honor to report that the enemy fired two shots over us at sunset yesterday, having done that he respectfully dropped his flag at the report of our evening gun.

There are in sight this morning the "Ironsides," four monitors, two wooden gunboats, three tugs, two mortar boats, and fifteen sailing vessels inside; three blockaders and one schooner outside, and fifteen vessels in Lighthouse Inlet. The "Wabash" has shifted her position a quarter of a mile more to northward and eastward of the lightship. I presume she dragged during the blow last night.

FORT SUMTER, January 2, 1864.

I have the honor to report that the vessels in sight this morning are the "Ironsides," four monitors, two wooden gunboats, two mortar boats, and fourteen sailing vessels inside. Three blockaders and two schooners outside, and thirteen vessels in Lighthouse Inlet. This is the smallest number that I have yet reported. Some parties are at work near Wagner this morning.

The 8-inch Columbiad was placed on the berm yesterday afternoon, it can be removed by a flat to-night.

FORT SUMTER, January 3, 1864.

I have the honor to report that Captain Adams, with six (6) officers and one hundred (100) men from the 6th, 19th, 23d, and 28th Ga., relieved Captain Botts, six (6) officers and one hundred (100) men from Ga. Vols. The "Ironsides," four (4) monitors, two (2) mortar boats, four (4) wooden gunboats (one of which I have not seen before), three (3) tugs, and fourteen (14) sailing vessels are inside the bar to-day. Eleven (11) craft in Lighthouse Inlet. Three (3) blockaders in front, one (1) three-masted, one (1) tug, and two (2) schooners to the northeast, and one (1) large transport and one (1) schooner in the offing going southward.

I think that from riggers on the blockaders and on the two schooners referred to, there is surveying going on to the northward and eastward.

I will hereafter report not only the number, but the movements of vessels in sight.

Large flagstaff raised at Wagner yesterday. 24-pounder shipped last night. Too much sea on the north wall for shipment of 8-inch. Will do it first calm night if flat is sent.

FORT SUMTER, January 4, 1864.

I have the honor to report that the boom in front of the sea and eastern portions of the gorge faces was successfully laid last night, and that it remains in position. I think that an addition to its length of both extremities would be an improvement. While the work of laying was going on, Fort Johnson fired three shots in this direction. Fortunately no harm was done. I understand that the sentinel thought he saw and heard musketry at this post. As we had two steamers and a fleet of small boats here, the risk to property was very great. The batteries being near the telegraph office, I was able to check it before our range had been obtained.

I recommend that Fort Johnson be no longer included among our supporting batteries. The distance is too great, and the required adjustment of aim too nice for good results to be obtained; and the probability is that the effect upon the garrison will be more injurious than upon the enemy. The difficulty is not owing to any defect in the skill of our artillerists, but belongs to the nature of the case.

At four-twenty (4:20) A. M. this morning, the alarm signal was made by the navy guard-boat, which afterwards reported two (2) small boats and a monitor approaching. The parapet had been manned and was kept so until daylight, as the night was peculiarly favorable to an assault. No observations this morning. Weather thick.

FORT SUMTER, January 5, 1864.

I have the honor to report the "Ironsides," four (4) monitors, two (2) wooden gunboats, two (2) mortar boats, and fifteen (15) sailing vessels inside. Five steamers, seven schooners, and one steam derrick in Lighthouse Inlet; the latter has always been there, but has not heretofore been specially reported. Ships in the offing not visible; fog last night very thick; multiplied the sentinels by ten (10). Work going on on Morris Island, but apparently not in the way of any change. One of the crew of the guard-boat shot himself through the hand while at the wharf; injured part successfully removed by Major Rhett, surgeon in charge.

FORT SUMTER, January 6, 1864.

I have the honor to report the "Ironsides," four (4) monitors, two (2) wooden gunboats, two (2) mortar boats, one (1) armed three-masted, one (1) armed brig, and twelve (12) sailing vessels inside. The three-masted and brig are not steam vessels; they have been here for some little time, but have not been specially reported. There are five (5) blockaders in sight, and twelve (12) craft in Lighthouse Inlet. Captain Groves, with six (6) officers and one hundred (100) men from 19th, 23d, 27th, and 28th Ga., relieved Capt. Tidwell, six (6) officers and one hundred (100) men from 6th, 19th, 27th, and 28th Ga. 8-inch Columbiad was shipped to city. Mr. Mathewes revised and corrected adjustment of boom.

FORT SUMTER, January 7, 1864.

I have the honor to report the position and scenes of the fleet the same as yesterday. No event of importance has occurred since yesterday.

FORT SUMTER, January 8, 1864.

I have the honor to report the position of the fleet the same as yesterday. The enemy are busily engaged in repairing the chevaux-de-frise at Gregg.

FORT SUMTER, January 9, 1864.

I have the honor to report the " Ironsides," four (4) monitors, two (2) mortar boats, three (3) gunboats, two (2) tugs, and ten (10) sailing vessels inside this morning.

Only one steam blockader plainly visible outside, together with five sailing vessels. Eight schooners, five steamers, and the steam derrick in Lighthouse Inlet.

Affairs on Morris Island have not changed lately.

FORT SUMTER, January 10, 1864.

I have the honor to report that Captain J. B. Allston, six officers, and one hundred men, from 27th S. C. V., relieved Captain Hammond, six officers, and one hundred men from 25th S. C. V. The steamer left the wharf without a proper head of steam, and began drifting with the tide below the fort. Seeing that she ran great risk of being fired into by Sullivan's Island as well as by the enemy, I directed both the telegraphic and signal operators to call Sullivan's Island. They tried for twenty minutes, from 12:30 o'clock to 12:50, without success. At the end of this time the steamer had recovered her position abreast of the fort. The night was perfectly calm and clear, and there is no possible excuse for the neglect of the signals. From what I have seen of the working of this corps, I would respectfully suggest that efficiency would be more certainly secured if the punishment were inflicted upon the operator, who by proper attention can always insure the vigilance of the reporting sentinels. I understand that there is a want of operators for the military telegraph line, and that many stations are supplied, as Fort Sumter is, with only one officer. I would recommend that to each office one or more enlisted men may be assigned, who shall be instructed in the call for that office, which a person of ordinary aptness for such matters could learn in a few days. In this way the attention of the office could be aroused at any time, which will not be the case if left to the wakefulness of a single person. I have had frequent opportunities of observing the working of the system since my residence at this post, and am confident that the proposed plan will answer.

DEFENCE OF FORT SUMTER.

Three (3) blockading steamers this morning. In other respects report same as yesterday.

"Ironsides" kept revolving light going all night. 42-pounder was placed upon the berm yesterday evening, ready for shipment.

FORT SUMTER, January 11, 1864.

I have the honor to report that Lieutenant Kemper, with thirty-eight men, relieved Captain King, forty men, last night.

There are visible this morning the "Ironsides," three (3) monitors—the fourth may be concealed behind the other shipping—two (2) mortar boats, three (3) gunboats, ten (10) sailing vessels inside. Two (2) steam blockaders and four (4) sailing vessels outside, and eight (8) sailing vessels and six (6) steamers in Lighthouse Inlet. Yesterday afternoon the 30-pounders at Gregg fired nine (9) shots, seven (7) of which struck.

FORT SUMTER, January 12, 1864.

I have the honor to report that the thick weather will not permit an observation of the fleet this morning. I was unable to discover the fourth monitor yesterday. A quantity of old iron was shipped by the steamer last night. A 42-pounder lies ready for shipment when the flat shall be sent.

FORT SUMTER, January 13, 1864.

I have the honor to report that nothing of importance has occurred since my last report, with the exception of the unmasking of one or more light Parrott guns than have heretofore been employed. They are situated at the foot of the scarps of the main work of Gregg. No observation can be made this morning.

FORT SUMTER, January 14, 1864.

I have the honor to report that affairs continue quiet. The density of the fog affords good cause for an assault, but it would not find us unprepared.

FORT SUMTER, January 15, 1864.

I have the honor to report that the weather will not permit an observation of the fleet this morning. Two (2) 42-pounder guns were shipped last night.

FORT SUMTER, January 16, 1864.

I have the honor to report that there are this morning inside: the "Ironsides," four (4) monitors, five (5) wooden gunboats, one (1) armed schooner, and one (1) armed bark, and ten (10) sailing vessels. The "Wabash" has given place to a small sloop of war without steam. In addition there are six (6) blockaders, two (2) without steam, seven (7) steamers, and ten (10) schooners in Lighthouse Inlet.

Private G. W. Duncan, Co. "E," 27th S. C. V., died suddenly yesterday of congestion of lungs and brain; also negro from the same cause.

FORT SUMTER, January 17, 1864.

I have the honor to report the "Ironsides," three (3) monitors, six (6) wooden gunboats, two (2) armed sailing vessels, twelve (12) unarmed, within the bar. The fourth (4th) monitor is probably concealed behind some of the other ships. The sailing sloop of war reported yesterday as having taken the place of the "Wabash" has moved inside, leaving four blockaders, two (2) of which are steamers. There are four (4) steamers and ten (10) schooners in Lighthouse Inlet. Four (4) shots were fired over the fort yesterday from one of the small Parrotts at Gregg.

FORT SUMTER, January 18, 1864.

I have the honor to report that Captain Johnson, six officers, and one hundred men, from the 19th, 23d, and 28th Ga., relieved Captain Groves with the same force.

Foggy this morning; no observations.

FORT SUMTER, January 20, 1864.

I have the honor to report the "Ironsides," four monitors, thirteen vessels, three of which are armed, one gunboat, and three tugs inside the bar; five blockaders outside, and seven schooners and five steamers in Lighthouse Inlet.

FORT SUMTER, January 21, 1864.

I have the honor to report that I assumed command of this post last night. No change in the fleet. Two (2) shots, Parrotts, fired at the fort, both of which missed.

    (Signed,) F. T. MILES,
           Captain Commanding.

DEFENCE OF FORT SUMTER. 163

FORT SUMTER, January 22, 1864.

I have the honor to report that Captain Burgess, five (5) officers, and one hundred (100) men from the 25th S. C. V., relieved Captain Allston, six (6) officers, and one hundred (100) men from the 27th S. C. V. There is one officer wanting to make up the regular detail. A steam tug was seen unusually near Fort Moultrie last night, retiring only at daylight. One shot fired yesterday, which missed. The water boat was not down. We stand in much need of the lanterns, for which requisition has already been made.

FORT SUMTER, January 23, 1864.

I have the honor to report that two (2) steam tugs of the enemy were stationed off the fort during the whole night. Number of fleet as usual. Water boat failed to come again last night. One shot fired, which missed.

FORT SUMTER, January 24, 1864.

I have the honor to report no difference in the number of the fleet. Seven shots were fired at the fort yesterday, three (3) of which missed.

I would respectfully suggest that all loaded shells be gathered together, and that men be sent here to extract the fuses to prevent accidents.

FORT SUMTER, January 25, 1864.

I have the honor to report some activity in the fleet this morning. A steam tug, and two (2) monitors were stationed at a short distance from the fort during night. One monitor still this side of buoy off Cummings Point.

I have the honor to request that another lieutenant from the 25th S. C. Vols., be ordered to report here for duty, as the second detachment of same regiment at this post wants one to make up the complement. I would respectfully refer you to the morning report of the 22d inst., in which I stated the want of one officer to make up the regular detail.

FORT SUMTER, January 26, 1864.

I have the honor to report that Captain Calhoun, one (1) officer, and forty (40) enlisted men from Co. "A," Lucas Battalion, Regular Artillery, relieved Lieutenant Kemper commanding, one (1) officer, and forty-five (45) enlisted men last night.

Number of fleet remains the same.

FORT SUMTER, January 27, 1864.

I have the honor to report that Captain Culpepper and seven (7) officers, and one hundred, (100) enlisted men from Colquitt's Brigade, relieved last night Captain Elliott, six (6) officers, and one hundred (100) enlisted men from same brigade. Two (2) shots fired at the fort yesterday, one of which missed. Too hazy to see fleet.

FORT SUMTER, January 27, 1864.

I have the honor to report my return to duty at this post.
(Signed,) S. ELLIOTT,
Lieutenant-Colonel Commanding.

FORT SUMTER, January 28, 1864.

I have the honor to report that I returned to the post last night, and resumed command this morning. Two (2) 32-pounders were shipped to the city last night. Three (3) shots were fired at the fort yesterday, and two (2) last night—all struck. During my absence, the parade, from which much of the water has been removed by evaporation, has been in a great measure covered with brick and lime. This is an improvement for the present in the sanitary condition of the work.

FORT SUMTER, January 29, 1864.

I have the honor to report that at 9 P. M., last night, the enemy opened on us with mortars from the middle battery, throwing by morning one hundred and twenty-three (123) shots, of which eighty-two (82) burst in and over the fort. Two (2) Parrott shots also struck.

I ordered the steamer to return to the city before her cargo had been entirely discharged, as she was in evident danger.

No injury was done to the work, and no casualties occurred. The firing continues this morning from guns. The thick weather obscures the fleet.

A tug was lying very close in at daylight this morning. I think she could have been struck by Sullivan's Island guns.

The fire is from three (3) 10-inch Columbiads, and a 30-pounder Parrott; is directed at the south angle where some open arches have been recently filled from the outside, and which we suspect they have seen. Work going on as usual and no damage done.

11 P. M.—Shots fired from 10-inch Columbiads, 8-inch Parrott,

6-inch Parrott, 40 and 30-pounder Parrotts at south angle, one hundred and fifty-six; one hundred and twenty-nine hit.

Mortar shells fired thirteen; seven hit.

Damage trifling. Casualties one man wounded in ankle.

FORT SUMTER, January 30, 1864.

I have the honor to report the "Ironsides," four (4) monitors, two (2) gunboats, two (2) tugs, fourteen (14) sailing vessels inside. The "Wabash" and six (6) blockaders outside. Five (5) steamers and ten (10) schooners in Lighthouse Inlet.

Fire direct on the west angle from 100 and 200-pounder at Gregg, and 100-pounder at the middle battery, probably the gun formerly used against the city. A garrison gun is now stationed in the adjoining embrasure.

Number of shots fired since morning one hundred and fifty-nine (159), hit one hundred and thirty-eight (138), missed twenty-one (21). West angle much cut.

FORT SUMTER, January 30, 1864.

At daylight yesterday enemy commenced his fire with a 30-pounder, a 100-pounder, and a 200-pounder Parrott, and a 10-inch Columbiad; one hundred and fifty-six shots were fired, one hundred and twenty-nine of which struck. The south angle was the object of their aim. An hour's work at dark repaired injury received. At 3 P. M. the flagstaff was shot down; it was first replaced upon a small, and afterwards upon a larger staff by Private F. Shafer, Co. "A," Lucas Battalion, who stood on the top of the traverse, and repeatedly waved the flag in the sight of the enemy. He was assisted by Corporal Brassinham and Private Charles Banks of the same corps, and by Mr. H. B. Middleton of the Signal Corps, who is acting as adjutant of the post in the absence of the regular officer. They were exposed to a rapid and accurate fire of shells. At the close of the scene Shafer, springing from the cloud of smoke and dust of a bursting shell, stood long waving his hat in triumph. It was a most gallant deed, and the effect upon the garrison was most inspiring. Thirteen mortar shells were also fired, seven of which struck. At dark the bombardment ceased. The steamer arrived with troops, stores, lumber, and sand. Captain Morrison, with six officers and one hundred men, from Colquitt's Brigade, relieved Captain Johnson's detachment. Two old 32-pounder casemate carriages were shipped to city. The fire has been resumed this morning, but is directed mainly at the west angle.

The following persons have been wounded: On night of 28th, Lieutenant J. L. Logan, head, by brick, slight. 29th.—Private J. H. Heffery, Co. "I," 23d Ga., contused back, slight.

FORT SUMTER, January 31, 1864.

I have the honor to report that there was no firing last night. It was resumed this morning as usual. A heavy cargo of sand and lumber was discharged last night.

A 42-pounder was placed in the northwest casemate ready to be mounted; a second with cracked band is half-way up the slope, and will be on the berm to-day for shipment to-morrow night.

FORT SUMTER, January 31, 1864.

I have the honor to report that the firing was continued to-day from the 200-pounder at Gregg, and from a 100-pounder in position where the gun was observed yesterday. It was directed against the southwest angle, which is a good deal cut. Much of the work done on it last night still remains. Number of shots one hundred and thirty-one (131), hit, one hundred and fourteen (114), missed, seventeen (17). The fleet is unchanged except in the absence of two (2) blockaders.

The nearest monitor was observed to have beams projecting from the sides similarly to the "Ironsides."

No casualties.

A Condensed Statement of the condition of Batteries Wagner and Gregg, Morris Island, S. C., from July 14 to September 7, 1863, compiled from original reports found among the papers of General G. T. Beauregard, by Lieutenant Ed. N. Kirk Talcott, 1st Regiment New York Volunteer Engineers.

July 14, 1863.—General W. B. Taliaferro assumes command of Morris Island, and reports the enemy throwing up works for siege guns on a line with Hospital Hill.

July 23.—General Johnson Hagood reports the effective force upon Morris Island to be, at Battery Gregg, 193 men; at Battery Wagner, 1,251 men. Total 1,444 men, mostly fresh troops.

The armament of Battery Wagner is reported to consist of one 10-inch Columbiad in good order; one smooth bore 32-pounder; one carronade, 42-pounder; two naval 8-inch shell guns; three 32-pounder carronades; one 10-inch mortar; two 32-pounder siege howitzers; two 12-pounder bronze howitzers.

July 26.—General A. H. Colquitt, commanding, reports the garrison on Morris Island, reduced to 1,000 men. A 32-pounder smooth bore gun was moved from sea to land face of Battery Wagner, and an 8-inch howitzer placed on the right flank of the work, replacing a 32-pounder carronade, dismounted on the 25th by a monitor shot. During the existence of a flag of truce, a torpedo in front of the battery was exploded by their own men, killing two of them.

July 27.—The 10-inch gun on the water-face of Wagner was disabled by a shot from the enemy, leaving but one gun upon the sea-face. The injury inflicted upon the fort was easily repaired during night.

July 28.—A mortar shell from the enemy exploded under the platform of an 8-inch shell gun, destroying the platform but not injuring the gun. Damage repaired the same day. An 8-inch S. C. howitzer was mounted on the flank curtain.

July 30.—J. M. Schueile, A. A. A. G., reports the armament of Battery Gregg in good condition save the left 10-inch gun, which lacks an elevating screw. The garrison is not at all under control of their officers. Batteries Wagner and Gregg were uninjured by to-day's bombardment.

August 1.—Colonel L. M. Keitt, commanding, reports the strength of the garrison of Morris Island at 1,600 effective men.

August 2.—The effect of the firing yesterday upon Battery Wagner was to make one large hole in the south end of the bomb-proof, and damage somewhat the land parapet, both of which are now repaired. The steamer "Chesterfield" was fired upon to-night at Cummings Point, at a rocket signal from some of the enemy's boats, compelling her to return to the city. A number of casualties but no material damage done to the battery.

August 3.—Garrison of Morris Island 943 effective men ; 32-pounder on the sea-face of Battery Wagner in process of being dismounted. Steamer at Cummings Point again fired upon, the signal being given as before.

August 5.—Traverse near the sally-port of Battery Wagner nearly completed. Magazine No. 2, on the sea-face, reinforced. Left flanking position on the beach repaired. Two 10-inch Columbiads on the sea-face put in fighting order. Enemy's shell very annoying.

August 7.—General Johnson Hagood, commanding, reports a 32-pounder rifled and banded gun put in position on the sea-face, in place of a 32-pounder smooth bore in Battery Wagner. Garrison of the Island—Infantry 1,037, Artillery 239. Total 1,276 men.

August 8.—Effective garrison of Island—Infantry 717, Artillery 240, Cavalry 11. Total 968 men. No material damage done by the enemy's fire to-day.

August 12.—Colonel George P. Harrison, commanding, reports garrison of the Island—Infantry 944, Artillery 270, Cavalry 11, Sharpshooters 20. Total 1,245 men.

August 13.—Garrison of Morris Island—Infantry 857, Artillery 269, Cavalry 11. Total 1,137 men.

August 14.—Garrison of Morris Island—Infantry 847, Artillery 273, Cavalry 11. Total 1,131 men.

August 15.—Garrison of Morris Island—Infantry 860, Artillery 269, Cavalry 11. Total 1,140 men. In Battery Wagner, banquette treads, erected on front and rear faces, improving the defensive condition of the work. Mortar bed at Battery Gregg cracked in both cheeks.

August 16.—Colonel Keitt, commanding, reports the firing from e enemy last night heavy, but doing but little damage to the work.

CONDENSED STATEMENT. 169

August 17.—C. L. Hill, Ordnance Officer, reports of Battery Wagner after the bombardment as follows: " Magazine *A* in perfect condition; a hole on the left of two or three feet, the only indication of injury to the parapet. Magazine *B* in perfect order. Parapet severely battered and very much uncovered. Magazine *C* in perfect order; one hole of five or six feet in parapet."

Lieutenant Alexander Gilson, Acting Engineer, reports after the bombardment, that "although a large amount of work will be required to repair the battery, yet the damage sustained by the bombardment is not of a very serious character. Neither of the magazines are materially injured, and the traverses can be easily repaired.

Captain Chichester, Chief of Artillery, calls attention to the fact that the enemy's batteries on Thomas Island* have a reverse fire on the gun chambers on the sea-face, and recommends that the traverses be thickened and heightened for protection. 8-inch naval shell gun No. 5, disabled by a Parrott shell.

August 18.—Chief of Artillery reports all the guns on the land-face of Battery Wagner uninjured, excepting one 32-pounder smooth bore, which has the carriage weakened. Rifled 32-pounder on sea-face disabled by a 15-inch shell. Left 10-inch Columbiad disabled (on sea-face). Working parties out all night repairing damages caused by yesterday's bombardment.

August 21.—Colonel Keitt, commanding, reports 12-pounder howtzer at Cummings Point disabled by enemy's shot. Guns now on sea-face of Battery Wagner are one smooth bore 32-pounder, protected by a traverse; one 10-inch Columbiad, traversing gear somewhat out of order; one 10-inch Columbiad useless. The land guns can all be fired, though two carriages are badly damaged. Magazines and bomb-proof are safe. Spiked plank were to-day placed in the moat. The greatest danger to Fort Wagner is from the enemy's skilful engineer approaches.

Captain Gregorie reports on the condition of Battery Wagner: "The parapets of this work are in as good condition to-day as at any time since I have been on duty at the post. I consider all the magazines and bomb-proofs secure from direct or vertical fire, the guns all in working order except the 10-inch Columbiad in the northernmost chamber. It requires a working party of 200 men every night and 1,000 sand bags to keep the fort up to its present standard."

August 22.—Captain Gregorie, Engineer, reports repairs last night

---

* Black Island.

on sea-face, which was badly torn up by the "Ironsides;" also traverse over southeast magazine was nearly cut through. Repaired embrasure on salient, and erected merlons for the protection of the men at the guns. Commenced traverse below the door of the southwest magazine.

Armament of Battery Wagner, August 21, was as follows:

No. 1. 32-pounder carronade at western gorge, in good working order.
No. 2. 8-inch siege howitzer on land-face, in good working order.
No. 3. 32-pounder carronade on land-face, in good working order.
No. 4. 32-pounder carronade on land-face, in good working order.
No. 5. 8-inch naval shell gun on land-face. Carriage very much injured by fragment of shell, but can be worked in an assault.
No. 6. 32-pounder smooth bore on land-face. Carriage much injured by fragment of shell, but can be worked in an assault.
No. 7. 32-pounder smooth bore on land-face, in good working order.
No. 8. 8-inch naval shell gun on land-face, in good working order.
No. 9. 42-pounder carronade on land-face, in good working order.
No. 10. 8-inch siege howitzer on land-face in salient, in good working order.
No. 11 32-pounder smooth bore on sea-face, to bear upon the beach, in good working order.
No. 12. 10-inch Columbiad on sea-face, to bear upon the beach, in good working order.
No. 13. 10-inch Columbiad on sea-face, unserviceable chassis, disabled by the bursting of a 15-inch shell.
No. 14. 8-inch sea-coast howitzer on curtain outside of rear gorge bearing on the land, in good working order.

In addition to the above, there is a 10-inch sea-coast mortar on the land curtain, near the western gorge, in good working order. Also two 12-pounder brass howitzers, on the curtain outside the rear gorge bearing on the beach.

Garrison of Morris Island Aug. 21 —Infantry 794, Artillery 240, Cavalry 10, Sharpshooters 14. Total, 1,058 men.

August 23.—General Hagood, commanding, reports that the car-

---

* The guns specified as "on land-face," or "to bear upon the beach," or "bearing on land," were intended to sweep, and did sweep the narrow strip of low beach, sometimes overflown by the tide, upon which all our approaches were run.—Q. A. G.

riages of both 8-inch shell guns are almost disabled, and can only be used in case of emergency.

August 24.—Southwest flank of Battery Wagner repaired. A new 6-pounder howitzer mounted on land-face. The remaining 8-inch siege howitzer dismounted.

August 26.—Colonel George P. Harrison, commanding, reports the garrison of the Island at Infantry 824, Calvary 10, Artillery 217. Total 1,051 men. Also capture of the rifle-pits in front of Battery Wagner by the enemy.

August 27.—Garrison of the Island—Infantry 1,381, Artillery 142, Cavalry 10, Sharpshooters 14. Total 1,546 men. Excuses himself for not attempting to retake the rifle-pits last evening because of the presence of torpedoes, planted by themselves in front of Battery Wagner.

August 29.—General Colquitt, commanding, reports the garrison of the Island—Infantry 1,123, Artillery 161, Cavalry 11, Sharpshooters 13. Total 1,308 men. The 9-inch Dahlgren gun at Gregg dismounted by a shot from the enemy's land battery.

August 30.—Garrison of Morris Island—Infantry 1,339, Artillery 152, Cavalry 10, Sharpshooters 18. Total 1,519 men.

August 31.—Steamer "Sumter" sunk by batteries on Sullivan's Island while taking troops from Cummings Point to Charleston. Garrison of Morris Island—Infantry 1,183, Artillery 195, Cavalry 10, Sharpshooters 16. Total 1,414 men.

September 1.—Garrison of Morris Island—Infantry 1,371, Artillery 204, Cavalry 10, Sharpshooters 16. Total 1,601 men.

September 2.—Garrison—Infantry 1,326, Artillery 195, Cavalry 20, Sharpshooters 25. Total 1,566 men.

September 3.—Colonel Keitt reports torpedoes planted in front of Battery Wagner, one being exploded by one of his own men.

September 5.—Colonel Keitt, commanding, reports a heavy bombardment from land batteries and gunboats, damaging the works materially, knocking sand from the bomb-proof and traverse in front of the stairs on left salient, leading to magazine and bomb-proof.

September 6.—Colonel Keitt reports that the enemy have breached the hills, and are knocking away the bomb-proof, and that by night their parallels will have reached the moat of the work, and urges immediate preparation for the evacuation of Morris Island.

September 7.—Colonel Keitt reports the successful evacuation of Battery Wagner and Morris Island.

The foregoing condensed statement is simply intended to indicate the number of troops maintained by the enemy on the north end of Morris Island.

The total force under General Beauregard's command did not vary much from 25,000 men, so located that they could all be concentrated at Charleston in a few hours' notice. From 5,000 to 7,000 men were kept in and near the works defending Charleston.

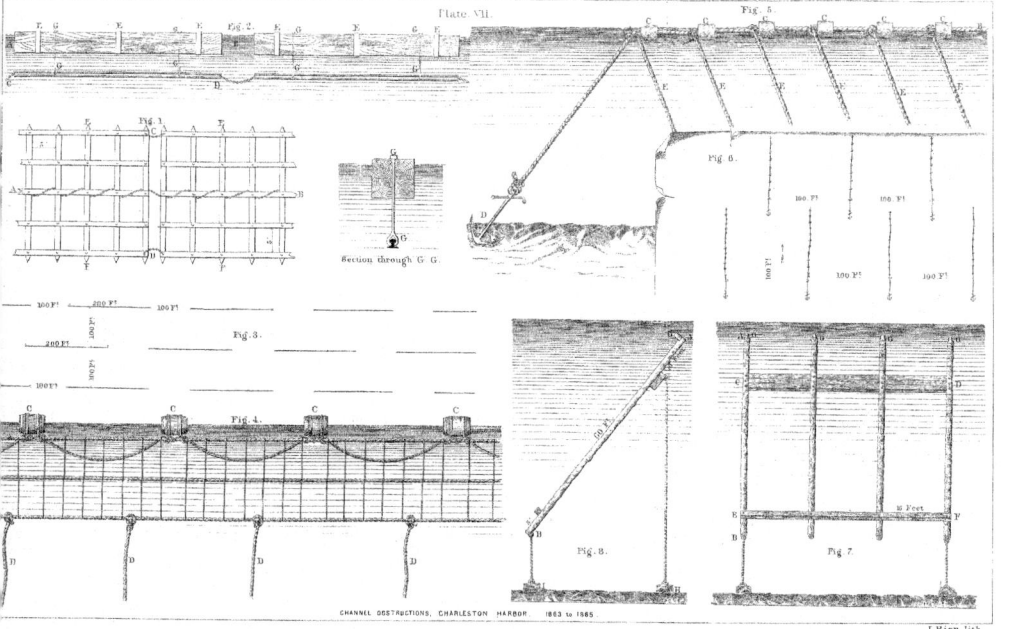